D0806686

101 Things
For Kids To Do Outside

101 Things
For Kids To Do Outside

DAWN ISAAC

PHOTOGRAPHY BY WILL HEAP

Kyle Books

First published in Great Britain in 2014 by Kyle Books
an imprint of Kyle Cathie Ltd.
67–69 Whitfield Street, London, W1T 4HF
general.enquiries@kylebooks.com
www.kylebooks.com

ISBN: 978-0-85783-183-5

Text © 2014 Dawn Isaac
Photographs © 2014 Will Heap*
Design © 2014 Kyle Books

All rights reserved. No reproduction, copy or transmission of this
publication may be made without written permission. No paragraph of
this publication may be reproduced, copied or transmitted save with
written permission or in accordance with the provision of the Copyright
Act 1956 (as amended). Any person who does any unauthorised act in
relation to this publication may be liable to criminal prosecution and civil
claims for damages.

Editor: Catharine Robertson
Designer: Louise Leffler
Photographer: Will Heap
Illustrations: Sarah Leuzzi
Copy editor: Liz Lemal
Proofreader: Helena Caldon
Index: Vanessa Bird
Production: Lisa Pinnell

Dawn Isaac is hereby identified as the author of this work in accordance
with Section 77 of the Copyright, Designs and Patents Act 1988.

A Cataloguing In Publication record for this title is available from the
British Library.

Colour reproduction by ALTA London.
Printed and bound in China

LANCASHIRE COUNTY LIBRARY	
3011812852525 4	
Askews & Holts	24-Feb-2014
796.083 ISA	£14.99
ML2	

* except photographs on pp.5 (bottom right), 11, 14, 38 (bottom right),
52 (left), 67 (bottom right), 80, 116, 122 (top middle), 133, 142 (bottom
right), 155, 156, 160, 170-171, 191 (bottom right), 199, 201, 202, 204,
215 (left), 216 (bottom right), 218 (right), 219 (middle) © Dawn Isaac

Sweep for bugs

Set up a potion lab

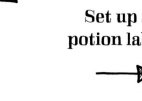

Plant an alpine colander

Play water balloon toss

Take the matchbox challenge

Fly a home-made kite

Hold a mini Olympics

Go pond dipping

Build a mud pie kitchen

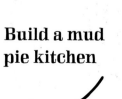

Build a snow lantern

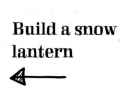

Contents

About this book

I could tell you that my family begins every day with a trek through the woods and ends it by singing songs round a campfire. I could tell you that but it would be a BIG FAT LIE. And, if you are that sort of family, why on earth are you sitting around reading this book? There are bear traps waiting to be set and animal calls to practise.

Right. Who's left?

Good. This book is for you.

It's for those kids who like TV, movies, popcorn, lying in bed, wallowing in baths, hanging upside down off the sofa for no good reason and staying in pyjamas all day. You see, you're the ones who need to get out a bit more. You're the ones who suddenly realise it's five to six on Sunday evening and you haven't left the house ALL weekend. You're the ones who are so pale it's very difficult to see you when you sleep between white sheets.

And, when your parents gently suggest you might want to go outside for a few minutes, this book is to stop you moaning 'But there's nothing to do outside'. Because guess what? There is. In fact, there are at least 101 things. I know because I've written them down.

So get outside. Race snails. Make potions. Go on a scavenger hunt. Plant a potato tower. Get soaking wet.

You can even do these things whilst still wearing pyjamas. What do I care? I don't have to wash them.

Your parents are going to love me!

Weave a bird's nest

YOU WILL NEED:
BENDY TWIGS, SCISSORS, STRING OR TWINE, STRAW, GRASS AND/OR FEATHERS

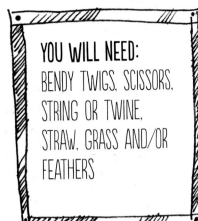

Why not try being a bird for a day? You probably shouldn't attempt flights off the garage roof, or sitting on high branches and singing at 5am (grown-ups tend to frown on such things), but you could have a go at weaving a nest.

You will need to collect six long twigs and cut them to about 40cm long (twigs from climbing plants are ideal as most bend very easily).

Cross the twigs over each other in a sort of star shape and tie them firmly together in the middle with string or twine to make the basic frame for the nest. Then weave in other long, soft twigs over and under the frame in circles, pushing the woven twigs towards the centre as you go.

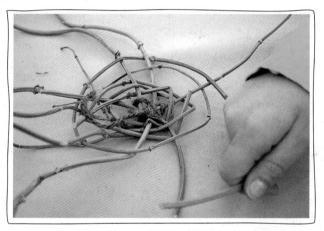

As you weave in more lengths, gradually pull up the twigs that form the frame to make the sides of the nest (you might need help from a competent grown-up for this part – WARNING: not all grown-ups are competent).

When you have worked your way up to the top of the nest, fill in the gaps by weaving in straw, long blades of grass or feathers.

After you have finished weaving, you can cut off the string at the centre of the frame.

Take the matchbox challenge

YOU WILL NEED:
EMPTY MATCHBOXES
(ELVES ARE OPTIONAL)

Never play with matches! Thankfully, empty matchboxes are a lot less dangerous and should be played with at every possible opportunity.

As well as making nifty drawers for elves, they are perfect containers for a miniature treasure hunt.

Make sure every player has an empty matchbox – all the same size. Giant matchboxes are definitely cheating (and are also too big for elves, in case you were wondering).

You have 15 minutes (or as long as you all decide) to fill your matchbox with as many things from the garden as you can find: a pebble, a leaf, a twig, a small feather, a blade of grass – whatever will fit in.

At the end of the game add up the points, one for each different item, and see who has won.

Tip: You can paint and decorate your matchboxes in advance to make them look more colourful.

12

 Use the smaller sempervivum rosettes to decorate the sides of the colander. It's easier to plant them if you make a hole with an old pencil first.

Plant an alpine colander

First you will need a colander. In case you don't know, this is a weird-looking bowl, riddled with holes, that's used to drain pasta or vegetables. You may also now realise that this can be quite useful, so best to check it's not needed for kitchen duty before you swipe it.

You can plant your colander with sedum and sempervivums. These are called 'succulent plants' because they store lots of water and so can go without drinking for a long time; a bit like camels, but smaller… and less grumpy.

Fill the colander with compost halfway up the sides and then place your sedum plants on the top before filling around the gaps with compost.

Next, take your sempervivum and carefully pull apart the different rosettes. Plant the larger ones in the top of the colander by making space for their roots with your finger and firming back the compost around them.

Use the strong runners of the smaller sempervivum rosettes (the bit of stem from which it's growing) to push through the holes around the top of the sides of the colander. It's easier if you use an old pencil to make the holes in the soil first.

Finally, place small decorative gravel around the plants in the top of the colander, to stop their leaves sitting on wet ground, before watering them. Even though they can put up with dry weather, keeping the plants regularly watered for the first few weeks will help them settle into their new home and start growing.

YOU WILL NEED:
COLANDER, COMPOST, SMALL SEMPERVIVUM AND SEDUM PLANTS, OLD PENCIL, GRAVEL

Learn semaphore

Tip: Put both flags in the downwards position to mark the end of each word.

Flag waving isn't just for sporting events and royal visits. No. You can also use it to tell your sister she smells whilst standing far enough away that she can't wallop you. Useful, eh?

To practise semaphore, you'll need to make a pair of flags each. First, get a piece of thin white A4 or letter-sized card, draw a diagonal line across it and paint or colour the lower section in black, or another dark colour. When it's dry, use a stapler or strong tape to join each piece of card to a stick or short bamboo pole.

Next, you and your friend each need to take a copy of the semaphore alphabet and go and stand a good distance apart. Start by practising all your letters to make sure they are easy for your partner to understand. When you're confident with this, you can start signalling messages to each other.

Tip: Try laminating the card before you attach it to the poles to make your flags waterproof and longer-lasting.

YOU WILL NEED:

THIN A4 OR LETTER-SIZED WHITE CARD, PENCIL, DARK PAINT OR COLOURED PENS, STAPLER OR STRONG TAPE, TWO POLES OR STICKS EACH, SEMAPHORE ALPHABET CHART, LAMINATOR AND POUCHES (OPTIONAL)

A B C D E F G H I

J K L M N O P Q R

S T U V W X Y Z

Try this for starters...

Tip: Unlike bricks, twigs are relatively easy to bend so you can make a curving or even circular fence with them.

Weave a twig fence

Tip: If you know anyone with trees, they often cut back 'suckers' from the base – these grow long and straight so are perfect for twig fences.

The story of the Three Little Pigs is all well and good, but how many parents do you know that'll let you build with bricks and mortar? Exactly.

Why not follow the example of pig number two and gather up some twigs and sticks? It might not save you from a ravenous wolf but you will be able to weave a pretty decent fence to keep out troublesome sisters or brothers.

First, gather a good selection of long sticks and twigs. You'll need to select the chunkiest for your fence supports and you may want to ask a grown-up to cut these to an equal size (ideally at least 60cm long).

Next, bang your supports in along the line of your fence. You could knock them in with a large stone, or a wooden or rubber mallet – just be careful to hold the stick a little way down so you hit the top of the wood, not your fingers. If you have long twigs, you could knock them in about 30cm apart. If you are dealing with shorter ones, you may find 20cm a better spacing.

Now you need to take your thinner twigs and weave them in and out of the twig uprights. Each time you have completed a run, push the twig down as far as it will go and right next to the twig before it so you don't have any big gaps. Make sure you alternate your weave each time so that if the last twig began behind the first upright, the next will begin in front of it.

YOU WILL NEED:
THICK STICKS/BRANCHES AND THINNER LONG TWIGS, STONE OR MALLET

Set up a potion lab

If you're a fan of Harry Potter, or simply want to channel your inner 'mad scientist', why not set up your very own potions lab outside?

First, set up your work surface: an outdoor table covered in a waterproof cloth works brilliantly. Next you'll need to find lots of different containers. As mad scientists tend to verge on the side of clumsy, it's probably safest to choose plastic vessels. It's also helpful to have a funnel, jugs and even the odd pipette or tweezers to hand – after all, dragon's blood and giant's snot call for some very careful handling.

Food colouring mixed with water will give your creations an interesting look, and for added fizz try adding a spoonful or two of bicarbonate of soda before splashing in a little vinegar. Other possible ingredients include stardust (glitter), rainbow essence (old poster paint), powdered unicorn bones (flour), statues' tears (rice) or monster slime (vegetable oil) – but always ask the grand high keeper of the kitchen for permission first (AKA your mum or dad).

When you've made your potions, decant them into small containers and add a helpful label (e.g. 'Shrinking Potion: not suitable for elves or goblins').

Just remember – DO NOT DRINK THE POTIONS! It won't end well.

Tip: For added authenticity try adding a white coat, safety glasses and demonic laugh (MWA, HA, HA). That should unnerve a few people.

Grow a potato tower

Have you ever sat on an old car tyre in the spring, holding a potato and wondering what to do next? No, I didn't think so. Still, if you ever find yourself in this position, here is the answer: build a potato tower.

First, you'll need to give those tyres a makeover. Put on some old clothes that you won't be yelled at for ruining, then lay some plastic on the ground or grass to protect it (an opened-up old compost bag works well). Get a thin layer of acrylic paint on a roller and apply it to the tyre. When it's dry you can recoat. It's best to build up a few thin layers rather than putting too much on at once.

Put your first tyre on some soil and fill it with potting compost. Next, take a potato. Ideally, this will be a proper 'seed potato' from a garden centre, but you could just use a spare potato from the weekly shop.

On the outside of the potato you should see little notches which look like someone's fingernail marks. These are called 'eyes' and this is where the potato will sprout shoots. Put the potato in the soil with the end with the most eyes pointing upwards. Next, put the second tyre on top of the first and fill with compost so the potato is buried about 15cm deep.

Keep the potato tower well watered in dry weather and in a few weeks you should see green shoots emerging. When these reach 15cm high, cover over with more compost, leaving only about 5cm showing. Keep doing this as the shoots grow, so you only leave 5cm of foliage showing, and add tyres on top as you need. Do this once or twice more (every two to three weeks) until your tower is three or four tyres high and the potato plant is in flower.

When all the flowers and leaves have died down, you can carefully pull back some of the earth and see if you can find any of the potato treasure hidden underground. You will be amazed by how many have grown.

YOU WILL NEED:
OLD CAR TYRES, OLD CLOTHES, PROTECTIVE PLASTIC SHEET (SUCH AS AN OPENED-OUT OLD COMPOST BAG), ACRYLIC PAINT, PAINT ROLLER, PAINT TRAY, NEWSPAPER, POTTING COMPOST, POTATO

Tip: So you don't use up too much compost, you can scrunch up some old newspapers and fill the tyre itself with these, then use the compost to fill the central hole.

A Scavenger List

feather

 fir cone

 seedhead

 stone with a hole

 strawberry

 daisy

 four-leaf clover

Warning: If your mum or dad add ten-legged spiders to the list, you know they don't want you coming back inside any time soon!

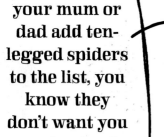 ten-legged spider

 rose petal

Hold a scavenger hunt

YOU WILL NEED:
A LIST, CONTAINER
OR BASKET

You can find all sorts of interesting things in the garden – balls, toy cars, lollipop sticks, juice cartons... Hang on a minute. Have you forgotten to tidy up *again*?

But even if you haven't been discarding your toys in all directions, there are still loads of things to find outside if you look hard enough, which makes it the perfect place for a scavenger hunt.

Ask a grown-up to write you a list of things to find in the garden, such as: feather, clover leaf, round pebble, rose petal, moss, strawberry, seedhead.

Then go out armed with a basket or container and try to collect as many as you can.

If there is more than one of you, it can be a race to see who finds them all first or who amasses the most in a certain amount of time.

This also works well for parties when you can divide into teams to look for the items.

Tip: To make it more challenging, the items can be quite specific. For example, a leaf with five points, a fluffy clematis seedhead or a seven-spotted ladybird.

Build a mini rockery

So when I say 'rocks' I'm really talking about cobblestones, but if we call this a 'cobblery' people will just look at you weirdly. And no one needs that.

First, clear a space on the soil in a sunny spot where your rockery will sit. Then place your largest stones in the area, mostly around the edge. Play around with them until you're happy with the look and then scoop out some earth beneath them so that the stones sit comfortably without wobbling.

Next, fill the space between and on top of the stones with potting compost. Keep adding more stones and compost so the structure is a good shape (narrowing towards the top), nice and stable and has plenty of compost-filled gaps.

When you've built the rockery structure, the next job is planting. Ideally, you should use alpine plants. These tend to be very small, low-growing plants, perfect for creeping over the stones. To plant them, simply scoop out some compost with your hands or a small trowel so all the roots of the plant will be underground, place in your plant, firm back the compost around it and give it a good watering.

Keep the rockery well watered for the first two or three weeks while the plants make themselves at home. Once they're happy they will clamber over and around the stones to create a pretty plant-filled 'cobblery' (that name might just catch on, you know).

YOU WILL NEED:
COBBLESTONES (CALL THEM ROCKS IF IT HELPS), POTTING COMPOST, ALPINE PLANTS, SMALL TROWEL (OPTIONAL)

Tip: Good plants to use include saxifrages, sedums, alpine varieties of campanula and aubretias.

Play skipping games

Tip: If you want to try out the long skipping rope games and you don't have enough people, tie one end of the rope to a strong post and you'll only need one 'turner'.

Skipping is a lot more fun if you play some games. These generally involve rhymes, and the important thing about these is they should make no sense whatsoever. That's right – none at all. Absolute gobbledegook if possible.

If anyone dares chant a rhyme that looks in danger of being sensible, do have words. They really are letting the side down.

YOU WILL NEED:
SKIPPING ROPE

Single skipping rhymes

'Jack be nimble, Jack be quick,
Jack jump over the candlestick,
mumble, kick, sizzler, split.
Pop-ups 10 to 1 – Hit it.
10,9,8,7,6,5,4,3,2,1'

Jack jump over – the jumper jumps up very high with both feet leaving the ground at the same time;

Mumble – put both feet together and make very small hops;

Kick – kick one foot outwards and back again;

Sizzler – cross and uncross feet and legs;

Split – open legs really wide and close again;

Pop – jump extra high with both feet coming off the ground together.

'Mabel, Mabel, set the table,
Just as fast as you are able,
Don't forget the vinegar, mustard,
and red-hot pepper!'

At 'pepper' turn the rope faster and faster until you can't keep up.

Group skipping (needs a longer rope)

'All in together girls
Never mind the weather girls
When I count 20
The rope must be empty'

(Try to leave the skipping without catching the rope and before the turners reach 20.)

'I had a little puppy
His name was Tiny Tim
I put him in the bathtub, to see if he could swim
He drank all the water, he ate a bar of soap
The next thing you know he had a bubble in his throat.
In came the doctor, (person jumps in)
In came the nurse, (person jumps in)
In came the lady with the alligator purse (person jumps in)
Out went the doctor (person jumps out)
Out went the nurse (person jumps out)
Out went the lady with the alligator purse (person jumps out)'

See. Told you.
Utter nonsense, every single one.

Tip: The herb garden should be in a sunny spot, but if you are going away on holiday and can't keep it watered, why not wheel the barrow into a shadier spot to stop it drying out too much before you return?

Plant a mobile herb garden

Wheelbarrows are terribly useful but do tend to involve a lot of work. So instead of using them to cart around bricks, move sand or shift earth, how about turning them into mobile herb gardens? It sounds a lot less tiring, doesn't it?

First, you need to find an old wheelbarrow – or at least one that nobody minds adding a few holes to. It's best to ask a grown-up to do this job by puncturing the base every 10–15cm with a large nail.

Next, give it a good brush out before filling it with some potting compost to within 5cm of the top. You can now start adding your herbs. Try to keep larger plants such as sage and lavender to the back or middle of the barrow where it's a little deeper. Also, if you want to add mint, make sure you keep it in its pot. Mint is a very bossy plant and will soon take over the whole barrow if you give it half a chance.

Some good herbs to try out are:

Marjoram or basil – great on pizzas, although basil will only grow outside in the warmer months

Chives – these have pretty purple round flowers and are good in potato salad

Thyme – low growing and very fragrant

Lavender – great for drying (see page 50) and making scented bags

Purple sage – lovely purple-grey leaves

Fill in around the herbs with gravel to keep the leaves from getting soggy and to give an attractive finish to your garden. Finally, give the barrow a good watering.

YOU WILL NEED:
AN OLD WHEELBARROW,
HAMMER AND NAIL
(GROWN-UP TO USE),
BRUSH, POTTING COMPOST,
HERB PLANTS, GRAVEL,
WATERING CAN

Tip: If you take a plastic folder with you, it will keep your paper and finished rubbings dry and stop them blowing away.

Make nature rubbings

YOU WILL NEED:
TREES, PAPER, WAX CRAYONS, MASKING TAPE (OPTIONAL), LAMINATING SHEETS AND LAMINATOR OR STICKY-BACKED PLASTIC (OPTIONAL), STRING (OPTIONAL)

Hug a tree if you like, but rubbing one is more interesting – and looks slightly less strange.

If you don't have lots of different trees in or around your garden, why not arm yourself with paper and crayons next time you go for a walk or visit a park?

First, have a look for some interesting bark. You'll see some trees have deep cracks, others are smoother or have lines around them. Next, hold your paper against the bark and use the side of your wax crayon to rub up and down. Keep the crayon nice and flat and the pressure even, and slowly you should see the pattern emerge on the paper.

If you are a natural fidget, you might want to secure the paper in place with masking tape or ask a friend to help hold it still.

You can use different colours each time or more than one colour in a single rubbing – whatever you think looks best. And why not try some leaves too? You can lay any you find on an outside table or flat surface, place your paper on top and rub away.

Tip: If you want to bring nature home with you then cut each rubbing into a large leaf shape, coat in sticky-backed plastic (or ask a grown-up to laminate them), add a hole and string them up as garden decorations.

Build a bird hide

Birds are nervous creatures, and as you might imagine, children running and screaming around a garden can make them a little anxious. So this is why, if you want to do any bird spotting, it can help to go undercover.

First, identify where the birds visit most often. This may well be by a feeder or bird bath. Next, you will need to set up your structure a couple of metres away. If you have any old tree branches you can use these to lean against each other, but it may be easier to place a few long bamboo canes in the ground and tie them together on the top to form a wigwam structure (see page 44).

Take your netting and tie it around the outside of the structure with some twine or string, leaving an entranceway (facing away from the bird feeder/bath).

Now take the plant and tree cuttings and weave them in and out of the net to camouflage the structure. Evergreen plants like ivies or conifers work well as they stay green for longer and keep their shape better. Keep going until you have covered the hide really well but make sure you leave a peephole on the side by the birdbath or feeder so you can spot the birds.

Now you just need to settle in place. It's a good idea to bring a stool to sit on as well as some binoculars and a spotting guide. And, if you plan to be there a while, a snack and drink wouldn't go amiss either.

Tip: Birds are also wary of change, so you may need to leave the hide for a day or two while they get used to it being there and come back to the feeder or bath.

YOU WILL NEED: TREE BRANCHES OR BAMBOO CANES, NETTING, TWINE OR STRING, FOLIAGE (CUTTINGS FROM TREES OR PLANTS), STOOL, BINOCULARS, BIRD-SPOTTING GUIDE, SNACKS (ALL OPTIONAL)

Grow a rainbow salad

Tip: If you don't have an area of soil you could do this in a very large pot or even a big old tyre filled with compost.

Eating up your greens can be so dull. However, eating up your oranges, purples, blues and yellows – well, that just sounds a whole lot more fun. So why not bring some colour to your meals by growing your very own rainbow salad wheel with colourful leaves and edible flowers?

First, in spring, prepare a circle of soil about a metre and a half across in a nice sunny part of the garden. Use a garden fork to turn over the soil, getting rid of any large stones and breaking down any big lumps by knocking them with the back of the fork until the soil looks nice and crumbly.

Use your stones to mark out the circle. To make an accurate shape, put a tent peg in the middle, tie on a piece of string and use a tape measure and craft scissors to cut the string to 70cm long. Now walk around the peg with it and use your path as a guide for placing your stones in a perfect circle.

Next, from the centre point, use the string as a guide to mark the six spokes of the wheel, again using your stones to form the lines.

Finally, sow or plant your colourful salad ingredients (see opposite) – one colour for each segment. You could try:

Red – Red nasturtiums (*Tropaeolum majus*), red pansies (*Viola* x *wittrockiana*) and Busy Lizzies (*Impatiens walleriana*), red-leaved lettuce

Orange – Orange nasturtiums, pot marigolds (*Calendula officinalis*), orange Busy Lizzies and pansies

Yellow – Yellow pot marigolds and pansies

Green – Lettuce (use lots of different varieties for a mix of textures)

Blue/indigo – Borage (*Borago officinalis*), cornflowers (*Centaurea cyanus*), blue pansies

Violet/purple – Purple lettuce, violet or purple pansies, sweet violets (*Viola odorata*), chives

YOU WILL NEED:

A GARDEN FORK, STONES, TENT PEG, STRING, TAPE MEASURE, CRAFT SCISSORS, SEEDS (SEE LIST ABOVE), WATERING CAN

marigolds   **purple pansies**

If you're sowing seed, do so in mid to late spring. Begin by drawing lines about 20cm apart in each segment using your finger or a stick. Now tip some seeds into one hand, then pick up a pinch of them between finger and thumb for small seeds (such as lettuce), or a seed at a time for bigger ones (such as nasturtiums) before carefully sowing them in the lines you have marked. Next, cover them over and then give them a good water (use a watering can with a fine rose so you don't wash the seeds away). Keep them well watered and seedlings should appear within a couple of weeks. If they are too close to one another, you can carefully pull some out to give the others more room to grow.

For Busy Lizzies and pansies, begin sowing in early spring in seed compost on a sunny windowsill (follow instructions on the seed packet) and plant them out after all danger of frosts has passed.

When flowers start to appear, harvest them with the lettuce leaves to create a rainbow salad.

Tip: In case the toys prove too good at hiding, make sure your grown-up remembers where they secreted them. If you've ever seen your mum or dad looking for the car keys you will understand how important this is.

Go on a bear hunt

No one to play hide and seek with? Don't worry, you can enlist the help of your soft toys.

First, select three of your favourite bears (or rabbits, dogs, dolphins – we don't want the other soft toys to feel left out). Then ask a grown-up to hide them around the garden while you stay inside, or just shut your eyes.

When the grown-up says they're ready you can start searching.

This may sound easy but, unlike brothers and sisters, soft toys are exceptionally good hide-and-seekers. They can stay very still and have never been known to giggle, sneeze or burp inadvertently. They are also a lot smaller.

In fact, why on earth did I suggest you go up against them? This is going to be very tricky.

On a positive note – when it comes to a rematch, you will undoubtedly win. They are absolutely appalling seekers.

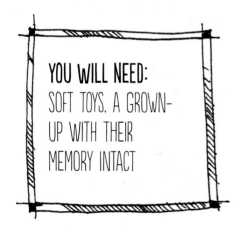

YOU WILL NEED:
SOFT TOYS, A GROWN-UP WITH THEIR MEMORY INTACT

Make a log walkway

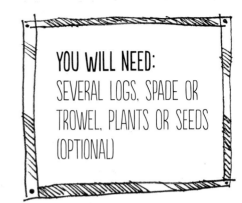

YOU WILL NEED:
SEVERAL LOGS, SPADE OR TROWEL, PLANTS OR SEEDS (OPTIONAL)

You may need to ask a grown-up to help you find some logs for this project. If they frown at the suggestion, try using some of the following arguments:

'A log walkway will improve my balance' (throw in a bit of a wobble at this point – it might help convince them).

'If I'm walking on the log walkway, I won't be walking on your flowers' (NOTE: only useful if they: a) have flowers in the garden; b) are used to seeing you walk on them).

'Building a log walkway will improve my construction skills and will probably lead to me being a world-famous engineer one day' (best said with a straight face, if possible).

Once you have convinced them of the need for some logs you can start planning the walkway. It can look good running through borders, or you can even use it as a secret pathway linking two areas of the garden (just make sure you agree the location with your grown-up first – or that frown may return).

If you have very wide logs, you could just place them in position on the earth, as long as you have compacted this down first to make sure it is firm and flat. Keep testing it as you go and checking the log doesn't rock or tilt as this can be dangerous. Also, make sure you are placing the logs near enough for you to reach them without overstretching.

Taller logs should be partly buried in the ground, so carefully dig down using a spade or trowel, flatten the base of your hole, put in the log and then ram the earth back firmly around it so it doesn't move.

Tip: It will make your log walkway blend in better and look more interesting if you plant up or sow in the earth around it. For a shady spot use ferns or woodland plants, or in a sunny place why not try sowing a wildflower seed mix?

Decorate the lawn

If you're holding a party or celebration outside, why don't you give the lawn a bit of a makeover?

First, you'll want to make sure it's just been cut (this is a job for a grown-up, and they're going to *love* the fact you keep nagging them to do it).

Next, you'll need to make some very large stencils. Old cereal boxes opened out or big packing boxes are perfect for the job. Draw on your shape and then carefully cut it out of the centre (you may need to ask a grown-up to help get you started).

Try to make sure the shape you are using is at least 30cm wide or tall, as anything smaller will be hard to see on the ground. It's a good idea to choose strong and simple shapes such as stars, crescent moons, hearts or perhaps a simple flower.

Next, lay your template on the lawn – you can keep it in place by putting stones around the edge – then simply sieve the flour over the template until it's thick enough to show up white on the grass.

When you have finished, carefully lift the template off the lawn and tip all the excess flour into a bowl to use again.

Tip: When the decoration is no longer needed, make sure you use a stiff brush to remove or spread the flour around before it rains

YOU WILL NEED:
LARGE PIECES OF CARDBOARD, PEN OR PENCIL, CRAFT SCISSORS, FLOUR, SIEVE

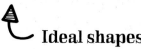
Ideal shapes

Plant a climbing bean wigwam

Isn't it great when an object has more than one use? A hammock can also serve as a pirate ship, a parent can make a good climbing frame and bean poles can create a perfect tepee-style den.

To make your own wigwam hideaway, you will need to find a circle of space about 1.5m in diameter in a nice sunny spot. Then mark out a circle. You can do this by using a tent peg to hold a piece of string, 60cm long, in the centre and then move it round to mark your circle using dry sand or small stones.

Next, take a piece of bamboo 60cm long and use this to mark six points along the edge of the circle. At each point push a 2.1m bamboo cane 30cm into the ground, leaning towards the centre (you may need a grown-up to help with this).

Tie all the bamboo poles together with twine, about 20cm from the top. If you can't reach, stand on some small steps or a chair, but check that it isn't wobbly first. You can then use more twine to add 'sides' to the tepee every 30cm up or so. Do this by weaving the twine in and around the poles and tying them at each end, leaving one gap open as a doorway.

Finally, plant a couple of beans at the base of each pole. These can be pushed in with your fingers until they are about 5cm under the ground. Water them in and wait. Within a couple of months the beanstalks will have reached the top of the poles and you will have a shady den to hide inside.

To make your bean wigwam

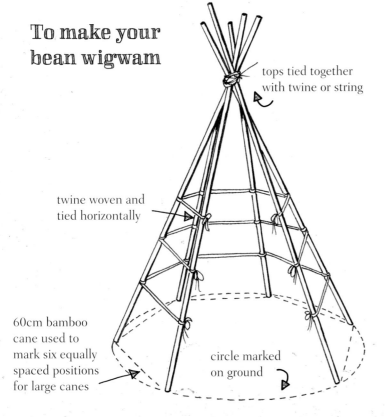

tops tied together with twine or string

twine woven and tied horizontally

60cm bamboo cane used to mark six equally spaced positions for large canes

circle marked on ground

YOU WILL NEED:
A TENT PEG, STRING, TAPE OR RULER (TO MEASURE YOUR STRING), STONES OR SAND TO MARK CIRCLE, 60CM BAMBOO CANE, SIX BAMBOO CANES 2.1M TALL, TWINE, BEANS TO PLANT

Tip: Don't plant your beans until you are sure there will be no more frosts as these can kill the plants.

Tip: If you don't have thick gardening gloves, you could use washing-up gloves that also have a good long sleeve

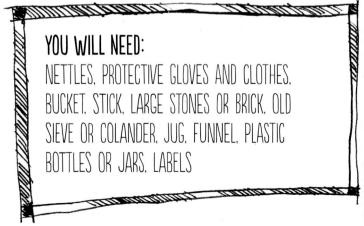

YOU WILL NEED:
NETTLES, PROTECTIVE GLOVES AND CLOTHES, BUCKET, STICK, LARGE STONES OR BRICK, OLD SIEVE OR COLANDER, JUG, FUNNEL, PLASTIC BOTTLES OR JARS, LABELS

Brew your own plant food

There are lots of reasons to make your own fertiliser: it gives plants, especially those in pots, a pick-me-up snack when they need it; it's cheaper than buying it in the shops; it's natural and, best of all, it really, REALLY stinks.

First, you'll need to find some nettles. You'll often see these in hedgerows, at the edge of fields, on wasteland and, if you forget to weed, in your own garden. To stop yourself being stung, make sure you wear thick gloves, a thick long-sleeved top, thick trousers and wellington boots.

Harvest the youngest, brightest green stems, as these will have the most nutrients. Either snip them off into your bucket or pull them up by hand. Try to fill a bucketful.

Now use a big stick or pole to bash and crush the stems and leaves in the bucket – this helps them break down quicker and release their goodness. Then weigh them down with a couple of large stones or a brick and fill your bucket three-quarters full with water. Rainwater is best, but tap water will do otherwise.

Leave your nettle concoction to brew. It will get smellier each day, so it's best to put it away from the house and outside seating areas – behind a shed or by a compost heap is a good plan. Make sure you can get to it to check on its progress. As it ferments, a foam will appear on top. When you see this, give the mixture a stir with a stick.

When it has finished fermenting (in one to three weeks), carefully strain it from one bucket to another through an old sieve or colander to get rid of the bits of leaves and stems. Now you can use a jug and a funnel to decant it into old plastic bottles or jars. Make sure you include the important information on a label – Nettle Tonic: dilute at a ratio of 1:10 with water and feed to plants. But there's no reason why you can't let your imagination go wild for your magic potion title – Simon's Stinky Solution, Pongtastic Plant Food, Will's Whiffy Wonder Tonic – you get the idea...

To use it yourself, pour a little of the tonic into a watering can and then dilute it by adding ten times as much water. Use this mixture to water the soil in the pots or around the plants to give them a boost.

Build a crawl tunnel

YOU WILL NEED:

OLD HULA HOOPS (ASK A GROWN-UP TO CUT THEM IN HALF), TWO 40CM LONG BAMBOO CANES FOR EACH HULA HOOP SECTION, TENT PEGS, WEED CONTROL FABRIC (OPTIONAL), PLAY SAND (OPTIONAL), NETTING, TWINE OR STRING, PLANTS, SEEDS OR FOLIAGE

There's nothing more fun than suddenly disappearing and then re-emerging when people least expect it. If you haven't quite mastered this magic act, then you may want to try creating a crawl tunnel – it does the same trick.

You can make your tunnel as short or as long as you wish – just remember, it can get quite tiring crawling around on hands and knees, so don't be too ambitious.

Insert the lengths of bamboo cane into the ends of your hula hoop sections so that half of the cane is still sticking out. You then push the bamboo parts of the hoop structure into the soil to make the entrance. Add more hoops in the same way every 30–40cm to create your tunnel.

To protect your knees, you can add a floor by cutting some weed control fabric the length of your tunnel and anchoring it to the ground using tent pegs. To make it softer still, you can even top it off with a layer of play sand.

You then need to attach some netting to the outside of your tunnel to give plants something to climb up. Lay the netting over the top and then tie to the hoops with twine or string and secure it to the ground using more tent pegs.

Finally, you need to cover your tunnel. If you want an immediate effect, you could tie or weave offcuts of branches or leaves to the netting. Otherwise, you could plant things which will grow over the tunnel.

If you're in a sunny spot and have good soil, you could try planting peas or beans around the base and let them climb up the netting (plant beans out after the danger of night frosts has passed, in late spring).

In shadier areas you could plant some ivy (choose varieties that won't get too big).

Also, many climbing plants, such as clematis or sweet peas, will be happy to crawl over netting.

Tip: Add curves to your tunnel to make it more interesting.

Harvest and dry herbs

Gardens are a little like gift shops. Only these ones don't charge. Yes, if you've got some plants growing, you can use your garden to make free presents for all sorts of occasions – Father's Day, birthdays, Christmas – without dipping into your precious pocket-money pot.

Herbs are particularly useful for this. You'll need to wait until the plants have got to a good size, but then they actually do better for a little bit of harvesting.

If you do want to cut some leaves, go out the evening before and check they look clean. If not, give them a quick rinse with a watering can (you don't want to wash them after you've harvested them or they'll be too damp and could go mouldy).

The best time to pick herbs is in the morning, once the dew has disappeared from the leaves. Yes, that's right, you're going to have to get out of bed for this one, but don't worry – just focus on those pocket-money savings.

The easiest way to dry most herbs is by hanging them, so go out and, using craft scissors, cut the stems. If these feel quite soft, it's most likely an annual herb and you can cut them to about half their length. If the stems are quite tough, it is probably a perennial herb (one that comes back each year) and it's best to cut only about a third of the stem off these. It's also ideal to cut herbs before they flower or, if it's lavender, when you can see the flower buds but they haven't opened.

When you've gathered some herbs, you need to use an elastic band to tie them together in small bunches (about five to seven stems in each). Then open up a paper clip from the middle so it forms a hook at both ends and slip one of them under the elastic band. Also remember to attach a label with the name of the plant as they can look very alike when they are dry.

The other end of the paper clip can be used to hook the bundles along a piece of string, hung like a washing line inside in a room or a playhouse that gets plenty of air but in a place that won't get direct sunlight.

Keep checking them and after two to four weeks they should be dry enough to take down. You can then strip off the leaves and put them into labelled, decorated jars as a gift. Dried mint leaves are great for teas. Lavender can be placed in a pretty bowl and used as a room scent like pot pourri. Sage, bay, thyme, marjoram and rosemary are very useful in the kitchen and so are perfect for keen cooks.

YOU WILL NEED:
HERBS, WATERING CAN, CRAFT SCISSORS,
ELASTIC BANDS, PAPER CLIPS, CARD OR
PAPER FOR LABELS, JARS

Tip: You can add to the woodland feel by finding moss to cover the base of the soil.

Make a twig plant pot

YOU WILL NEED:
A PLASTIC PLANT POT, TWO ELASTIC BANDS, TWIGS, TWINE, POTTING COMPOST, BULBS OR PLANT, MOSS (OPTIONAL)

Tip: For a colourful plant pot, why not use yellow or red dogwood or willow twigs? You can also use pussy willow stems for an interesting 'fluffy catkin' look.

Black plastic plant pots are many things: cheap, practical, easy to get hold of. Unfortunately, they are also pretty ugly.

If you want to give one a makeover, then forget hair and beauty products; all you need are a couple of elastic bands, some twine and an awful lot of twigs.

Begin by putting two elastic bands around the pot – one near the top, the other near the base. Then you need to find some twigs. You can look around the base of trees where you will often find discarded twigs. Just remember: don't break them off – trees and bushes need their twigs and will only discard those they're not using.

When you've gathered your twigs, snap them to a length just a little longer than the height of your pot. Then slip them, one at a time, beneath the two bands so they are held upright against the pot. Do this again and again until the black pot beneath is hidden by the twigs.

Finish off by wrapping twine around the elastic bands so it covers them and completes the natural outdoor look.

In autumn, it's a good idea to plant bulbs in your pot and leave them outside until the flowers emerge in spring. At other times of the year, you could fill your pot with small flowering plants.

Start a mini vegetable garden

You don't need a big garden to grow vegetables. In fact, you don't need a garden at all. All you really need is some kind of large container, compost, seeds… and some patience. Admittedly, that last one can prove tricky but keep searching – you might just find a little lying around.

All sorts of things can be used – an old wheelbarrow, a wooden crate, a baby bath (preferably without the baby), a plastic storage box. The most important things are that: a) it's no longer needed (see my previous point about the baby) and b) you can put some drainage holes in the bottom if it hasn't already got some.

You can ask a grown-up to help make some holes in your chosen container by knocking nails through it if it's made of metal, or drilling through it if it's made of plastic or wood. You can then line your 'garden' with some thick plastic (old compost bags work well) and make sure this also has small holes cut in it.

Next, put your container somewhere sunny and fill it up with potting compost until you're about 5cm from the top, firming it down as you go.

Now divide your 'garden' into beds – you could use sticks or shells to mark these out – before deciding what to sow. The most important thing is to choose relatively small plants and only sow a few seeds of each. Good choices include: 'Parmex' carrots, 'Tom Thumb' lettuces and radishes. If you write the name of each crop on a lollipop stick you will know which veg will appear where.

Remember to keep your garden well watered and harvest your crops when they are ripe.

> ### YOU WILL NEED:
> A LARGE CONTAINER (WITH DRAINAGE HOLES IN THE BOTTOM), THICK PLASTIC, POTTING COMPOST, STICKS/SHELLS/STONES FOR MARKING BEDS, SEEDS, WATERING CAN, PLANT LABELS OR LOLLIPOP STICKS, PEN

Paint with water

Not all art needs to be permanent. After all, there is only so much space on the fridge to stick the stuff. This is why water painting works so well. It is very much 'Now you see it, now you don't' art.

You can paint with water on anything that will go darker when it's wet – slabs, bricks, fences. And you can really use whichever tools suit you best. If you want a picture with more detail, try using finer brushes. Or if you want to make more of an impact, really wide paintbrushes or rollers work brilliantly. Just get a jar or tub of water, dip in your brush and get going.

Or why not take out a washing-up bowl of water and make a picture using hand- or even footprints?

If you want your picture to last longer, paint in a shadier area. Or if you want to challenge yourself to create a picture in record time, paint in a sunny spot and see if you can complete the work of art before it's evaporated into nothing.

You can also write a rude message to your brother and by the time your parents have come out to read it and tell you off, the evidence will be gone. Result.

YOU WILL NEED:
WATER, BRUSHES, ROLLERS (OPTIONAL), CONTAINER FOR WATER

Play tag games

'You're it.'

'No, you're it.'

'No, you're it.'

Sound familiar? Thankfully, there are some more interesting versions of this game which may stop the bickering. Here are a few.

Glue tag

When tagged, whoever is now 'it' has to keep a hand attached to the body part they were tagged on. The trick is to tag in as awkward a place as possible – an elbow or ankle works particularly well.

Stick in the mud

Once tagged by 'it' you must stay stuck in the mud – rooted to the spot, feet apart. Fellow players can release you by crawling through your legs. The only time you are safe from being tagged is when you're in the midst of releasing another player. This game can prove exhausting for 'it' if they have too many to tag, so a version can see any player who gets 'stuck in the mud' twice become an additional 'it' to help the tagging. The game ends when 'it' has stuck all players in the mud – or collapses in exhaustion.

Spider tag

The tagger is a 'spider' and all others are flies. When tagged a fly has to hold hands with the spider and race around trying to tag too. As more flies are caught in the web the chain gets longer and longer – perfect for cornering more flies and trapping them in the web. The winner is the last person caught, who then becomes the next 'spider'.

YOU WILL NEED: STRIPS OF CLOTH, HANKIES OR HEADSCARVES

Pickpocket tag

This game is perfect for training Fagin apprentices. To start, each player has a strip of material, hanky or headscarf to hang out of their back pocket or the waistband of trousers, skirt or shorts. The aim is to grab and capture as many of your fellow players' strips as possible. The winner is the one with the most at the end.

Plant a lettuce ball

Delicious!

If you hadn't already guessed, this is a ball for picking – not kicking. It's also the perfect way to keep slugs away from your lettuce leaves... unless they've learnt to fly (which they might well have done – slugs are very tricky like that).

It takes lots of salad leaf plants to make this ball. Lettuce grows really easily, so why not sow some in a seed tray filled with potting compost on a sunny windowsill in spring or summer? When the seedlings have grown large enough to handle (with a couple of good-sized leaves), you can carefully loosen the compost around their roots, lift them gently by the leaves, and plant them into a larger compost-filled pot. Within two to three weeks, they should be ready to plant.

You will need two hanging baskets – plastic-coated wire versions with a criss-cross pattern are perfect for the job. They will have three chains attached to each one – unhook all of these, but keep one close by as you are going to need to use it again. Because the baskets are round, they do tend to roll about, so it's best to balance them on a good-sized pot while you're planting them up outside.

Take a lettuce plant carefully out of its pot and gently wrap some paper around the leaves so that you can carefully thread this 'tube' through one of the holes in the side of the basket from the inside.

Next, add some moss around the base of the leaves inside the basket so you can't see the soil. Keep doing this until half of the main gaps are filled with salad leaves and all the others are covered in moss, and then top up the rest of the basket with compost, firming it down gently as you go.

Next, do the same with the other basket until they are both full.

At this point you need to very quickly turn one basket upside down on top of the other. You will need to get a pair of grown-up hands to help with this (preferably some attached to a body).

When the baskets are balanced on top of each other, reattach the chains by hooking them through the edges of both baskets so they finish in a hook above the top of the ball.

Finally, give the ball a very good watering before asking a grown-up to hang it from a special wall bracket or a strong hook attached to an outdoor porch or somewhere similar. You might even be able to hang it from a playhouse and at a height where you can reach it – but the slugs can't.

Then, when you fancy a salad, you can just carefully snip off some individual leaves. If you only take one or even two from each plant, they can grow more to replace them.

Tip: Make sure your lettuce plants are cut-and-come-again rather than head-forming varieties, so you can harvest individual leaves.

YOU WILL NEED:
LETTUCE SEEDS (OR SMALL PLANTS), SEED TRAY, PLANT POTS, TWO HANGING BASKETS, PAPER, POTTING COMPOST, MOSS, STRONG HOOK OR WALL BRACKET

To make your lettuce ball

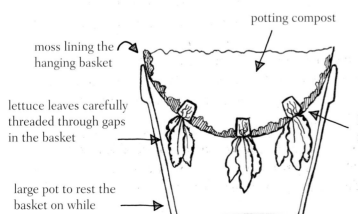

potting compost

moss lining the hanging basket

lettuce leaves carefully threaded through gaps in the basket

lettuce plant root ball

large pot to rest the basket on while planting

hooks connect the two baskets together

Tip: If you put half a teaspoon of sugar in your water, it will give any flowers that haven't opened up a little more energy to come into bloom.

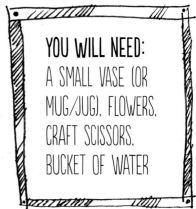

YOU WILL NEED:
A SMALL VASE (OR MUG/JUG), FLOWERS, CRAFT SCISSORS, BUCKET OF WATER

Arrange some flowers

It is worth learning, early on, the power of flowers. They can smooth over many a tricky situation: 'I'm sorry I paddled mud through the house/drew on Grandpa's face whilst he napped/gave the cat a haircut (delete as appropriate), but here – have this vase of flowers!'

You don't want to rob your garden of all its blooms but if you arrange them in a small container it doesn't take many flowers to make an impact.

First, you need a vase. Charity shops are a great place to pick up some pretty pots for only a few pence, or you can simply use a small jug or mug from the kitchen (just make sure you ask permission first, or you will simply be adding to the tricky situations list).

Choose flowers which complement your vase or just pick some of your favourite colours. Try to make sure you cut a decent length of stem, and it's a good idea to put the flowers in a small bucket of water to stop them wilting.

Tip: Try to change the water every two or three days to keep the flowers looking fresh

Arranging the flowers outside keeps mess to a minimum, but do make sure your water-filled vase has a nice flat surface to sit on.

Strip off the lower leaves or they will get soggy (and smelly) in the water and then recut the stem to a length that looks right in your vase (you may need to experiment with this). Using odd numbers of flowers, such as threes or fives, works well and don't forget that foliage plants look good alongside their petally friends.

Make outdoor bunting

Tip: You can add extra decorations to the plastic flags by drawing on them with acrylic paint pens.

Bunting makes almost anyone feel cheerful – except maybe a person who's just found out they have double maths on a Friday afternoon. Still, even in these circumstances, a few well-placed flags might help. Bunting is *that* powerful.

It's also very easy to make your own outside version. First, think about where you want your bunting to hang. Next, you will need to get some ribbon (or string) long enough to stretch between the two points with a little extra length to allow you to tie it up at either end.

Then get a thick piece of card and, using pencils and a ruler, make a large triangular shape. Cut this out and you have your template. Lay this on some colourful plastic bags or coloured cellophane and draw round the shape with a ballpoint pen. Cut out these flags and then fasten the top of each to your ribbon in three or four places with a stapler.

If you are using string, bend the top of the flag over the string line and staple the turnover in place. Decorate your bunting if you wish, and it's ready to hang.

YOU WILL NEED:
RIBBON (OR STRING), THICK CARD, PENCIL, RULER, CRAFT SCISSORS, THICK AND COLOURFUL PLASTIC BAGS (OR CELLOPHANE), PEN, STAPLER AND STAPLES

Grow and autograph a pumpkin

YOU WILL NEED:
A PLANT POT, POTTING COMPOST, PUMPKIN SEED, WELL-ROTTED MANURE OR GARDEN COMPOST, A SUNNY PLANTING SPOT IN THE GARDEN (OR LARGE POT), SPADE OR FORK, PEN

There are many places where you shouldn't write your name: on furniture, trees, anywhere on your body in permanent marker – and that's just for starters. However, pumpkins are a different matter. Grow your own this summer and practise your signature at the same time.

First, in late spring, fill a small plant pot with compost and put in a pumpkin seed, on its side, 2.5cm deep. Then give it a water and place it on a sunny windowsill, making sure the pot doesn't dry out.

By the time summer begins you should find that these seeds have grown into small plants which you can relocate outside. Choose a sunny, sheltered spot and make sure you feed your plant by digging some well-rotted manure or garden compost into the ground with a fork before planting the pumpkins.

When the pumpkins are about the size of a melon, you can write your name and draw pictures on them by pressing into the skin using an old pen – but make sure the nib only sticks in about 2mm. The pumpkin will form scar tissue over the markings and these will grow larger as the pumpkin does, leaving your signature for all to see.

Ask a grown-up to cut the pumpkin off with a long stalk before the first frost and it will keep indoors for up to six months.

Tip: Pumpkins are very large plants, but if you haven't much space, you can buy smaller varieties which grow happily in pots.

Tip: When the pumpkin has coloured up and the outside is hard enough not to be dented with a fingernail, it is ready to be harvested.

Play jingle jangle

You will not find this game easy. It involves a skill that has eluded children since time began. That's right. You have to be quiet. Told you it was hard.

Begin by blindfolding all the players except one. This person will need to have some bells attached to some string or ribbon tied around their ankles or wrists. For those of you who don't have a ready supply of ankle bells (really? no ankle bells? how odd!) then you could tie on some keys (just make sure you ask permission first).

The aim for the 'jangler' is to avoid capture. They can move away from the blindfolded players trying to catch them, but to do so may also give away where they are, as moving will make them jangle.

The first person to seize the jangler becomes the jangler themself. Alternatively, you can simply set a time limit on the game – if the jangler remains uncaught after five minutes, they win.

YOU WILL NEED:
BLINDFOLDS, BELLS
OR KEYS, STRING
OR RIBBON

The 'jangler'

The 'jangler'

Tip: Have a defined area for the game and a referee to keep blindfolded players out of danger and to make sure the jangler plays fair! To make the catching easier, limit the jangler to walking – no running allowed!

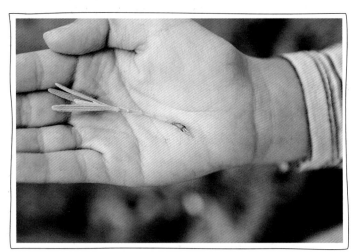

Tip: Try to take several 'pullings' to increase your chances of success.

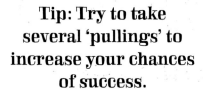

Make new plants

Sowing seeds is just one way to grow more plants for your garden. Many plants actually grow better from a little piece of shoot. Gardeners usually call this 'taking cuttings', but as we're not going to need any sharp objects we'll just call them 'pullings'.

First, you need to find a plant to use. Good ones to try are lavender, sage and rosemary – just make sure you ask permission from a grown-up before pulling bits off their plants. In the late spring or early summer have a look at the plant. You want to find a good side shoot – a piece growing off a bigger stem. Ones about 7–10cm long are best.

Take hold of the side shoot and remove it from the plant by pulling it downwards. Doing this should mean you take a tiny slither of the main shoot with it too. This is what gardeners call a 'heel', but as it looks very little like a heel and has nothing to do with shoes we might as well call it a 'thingamejigawhatsit'.

Plants lose water through their leaves and take water in through their roots. At this point you may realise that your 'pulling' has a few leaves but absolutely no root, so it's going to get a bit thirsty. To help it out, remove all the leaves from the bottom two-thirds of your 'pulling'. If you are taking a side shoot from a plant with really big leaves, you can even reduce the size of the leaves by cutting them in half with some scissors.

Now make a hole in the ground, or in a pot of potting compost, with your finger or an old pencil, and drop in the 'pulling' so only the top half is poking out. Finally, press the soil or compost down firmly around it and give it a good watering.

If you can keep the pulling shaded for a few days it will help to stop it drying out before it has a chance to grow roots. Also, make sure the compost or soil doesn't dry out.

If after two or three weeks the leaves are looking quite healthy, you can be pretty sure your pulling has very cleverly started to grow itself some new roots from its 'thingamejigawhatsit'. In a month or two it should start to grow new leaves and shoots. At this point you can give yourself a pat on the back – you've just created a new plant.

YOU WILL NEED:
A PLANT, CRAFT SCISSORS, OLD PENCIL, PLANT POT AND POTTING COMPOST (OPTIONAL)

Construct a water wall

It can be very entertaining pouring water, particularly over someone's head. However, it's almost as much fun (and a lot less likely to get you into trouble) if you build your own water wall to pour it into.

If you have a piece of trellis already fixed to a wall or fence, this makes the perfect base. If not, you could also use a piece of framed trellis propped up against a wall or even some strong wire mesh.

To make your water wall, you need to attach different pipes, tubes and containers to the trellis or mesh. Make sure the water can travel – for example, if you have an old bottle, you could cut off the base, take off the lid and turn it upside down to make a funnel. Alternatively, you can puncture holes in the base and let the water sprinkle out or even cut it lengthways to make a water slide.

An old piece of hosepipe cut into sections is a great way to direct water between different containers. To make it fit snugly into the neck of a bottle, attach it with plenty of strong duct tape to form a tight seal.

To secure all the bottles, pipes and tubes to the wall, thick, twistable, plastic plant ties work brilliantly, or you could use some plastic-coated garden wire or even pipe cleaners.

When it's all set up, pour water into the top parts using a jug and watch to see how the water travels. You can then adjust the water wall to make different routes and features. Also, place some buckets at the base so you can catch the water to use again in the wall.

YOU WILL NEED:
TRELLIS, AN OLD HOSEPIPE,
PLASTIC BOTTLES, PLANT TIES,
WATER, BUCKETS, JUG, ACRYLIC
PAINT PENS AND FOOD COLOURING
(OPTIONAL)

Tip: To brighten
up your water wall,
use acrylic pens
to decorate the
plastic bottles, or
add food colouring
to the water.

Hold a mini Olympics

The best thing about holding the Olympics in your own back garden is you avoid the lengthy bid process, there is no need to have representatives from 200 nations traipsing across your lawn and you can have them more often than once every four years.

And then there are the events. Whilst there's nothing wrong with a sprint, relay or long jump, these are your Olympics, so you needn't follow the rules of any international organising committee.

Feel free to adopt the longest frisbee throw, spacehopper relay race, hula hoop endurance event or lowest limbo.

If you have a mix of ages, you may need to divide some of the events by age ranges or impose a handicap system where players have time, point or distance penalties based on how old they are.

YOU WILL NEED:
LOTS OF COMPETITORS,
SCORING SHEET, PENCILS,
EQUIPMENT FOR SPECIALIST
RACES (E.G. FRISBEES,
HULA HOOPS), MEDALS
(OPTIONAL — YOU
CAN MAKE YOUR OWN),
PODIUMS (OPTIONAL)

Tip: For added authenticity, feel free to add medal ceremonies, flags and podiums. However, to avoid the need for the fire brigade, it's best to leave out the Olympic torch.

Why not set up an obstacle race?

To make your butterfly feeder:

Tip: To make your jar even more colourful, use brightly coloured twine rather than plain string.

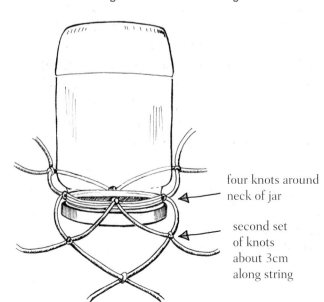

four knots around neck of jar

second set of knots about 3cm along string

YOU WILL NEED:
WATER, SUGAR, PAN (GROWN-UPS TO USE THIS), JAR WITH LID, ACRYLIC PENS, STRING OR TWINE, HAMMER AND NAIL (GROWN-UPS TO USE THESE), SPONGE OR COTTON WOOL

Make a butterfly feeder

Yum!

Butterflies are very like children. They are both more than happy just eating sugar. However, unlike children, butterflies can do this without running around like maniacs afterwards and feeling slightly ill.

So, why not use some sugar to set up a butterfly feeder in your garden and watch to see which butterflies visit?

First, ask a grown-up to make your sugar water. This is done by dissolving one tablespoon of sugar in nine tablespoons of water by heating it in a pan.

While that cools down, you can construct the feeder. Take a small jar and decorate it with brightly coloured flowers. You could tape on paper shapes, but it will last longer if you draw them on using acrylic paint pens.

Next, take your string or twine and cut four lengths at least three times longer than the jar itself. Take each piece and, making sure you have an equal length either side, tie it around the neck of the jar, finishing in a knot. Do the same with the next piece, this time making sure the knot is on the opposite side. The final two pieces should end with the knots halfway between the other two so that all four knots are equally spaced.

Now turn the jar upside down before taking a piece of string from each of two adjacent knots and tying them together about 3cm up the string. Do this with all the other pieces until you can see a net pattern forming. Repeat this with the second layer of knots and continue until you reach the top of the jar.

You will now need to add a hole to the jar lid. You can do this by hammering through a nail (which is best done by a grown-up). Next, take your small piece of sponge or cotton wool and thread it through the hole so some is poking out of both sides. It should be a snug fit so that the water soaks the sponge but doesn't drip off (you can experiment until you get it right).

Finally, fill the jar with the sugar water, put on the lid and use the string, bunched together, to hang it somewhere in the garden where the butterflies can see it – a sunny spot is best. Now see how many butterflies visit and if you can identify them all.

Build a human sundial

Having your own watch – that's OK. Being your own watch – now that's impressive.

It's also pretty easy. You'll just need a sunny piece of ground, a few stones or tiles and a small paving slab or a couple of bricks.

Oh, and you might need to get out of bed when the sun comes up, but let's not worry about that now...

To begin, head out at midday, when the sun will be at its highest point. Place your slab down and stand on it. You are now officially a gnomon. No, put away the fishing rod and silly hat, I didn't say 'gnome', I said 'gnomon' – otherwise known as the pointy-up-bit-on-a-sundial.

When you're standing nice and straight, look at your shadow. Wherever the top of it hits, you need to place a stone (or ask a friend to do it) – this is the topmost point of your sundial.

Next, set a timer so you know when it's one o'clock. As soon as it rings, run back to your slab, stand up straight and again place another stone where the top of your shadow hits.

Continue doing this on the hour, every hour, until the sun goes down. The next day, you can get up early and start again on the morning hours.

When you've finished you should have a roughly semi-circular pattern of stones forming your very own human sundial.

YOU WILL NEED:
A SLAB (OR BRICKS),
STONES OR TILES,
TIMER, ACRYLIC PAINT
AND BRUSH (OPTIONAL),
SUNSHINE

Tip: You can add lines of stones from the slab to the topmost stone to make the readings easier. You could also paint numbers or Roman numerals onto the top stones with acrylic paint.

Tip: Don't put more than two or three crabs in a bucket at a time, or mix big and small crabs, or they can start to fight.

Go crabbing

This is the perfect seaside activity. Well, OK, eating ice cream is the perfect seaside activity – but this comes a close second.

First, you'll need a bucket to place your crabs in. Fill this with seawater and add a rock and seaweed if you can to give the crabs somewhere to hide. Also, make sure you keep it out of the sun so they don't get overheated.

Now you need to get crabbing. Rock pools or harbours are good spots. Tie a little bait to the end of your string or line and then lower it gently into the water. Or you can use a little net bag to put the bait into and tie it to the end of the line instead.

Loop the line over your finger so you can feel when a crab 'bites'. When you think a crab has a good hold of the bait, start pulling up the line slowly and smoothly. If you have a fishing net, use this to scoop up the crab as it gets near the surface.

If you want to pick up a crab, hold either side of the shell, just behind the pincers, with your finger and thumb, so you don't get nipped. Make sure you put your crabs back in the water when you've finished looking at them, and don't keep them in your bucket for more than about an hour.

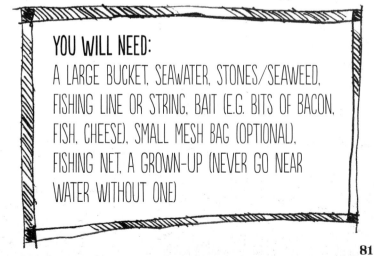

YOU WILL NEED:
A LARGE BUCKET, SEAWATER, STONES/SEAWEED, FISHING LINE OR STRING, BAIT (E.G. BITS OF BACON, FISH, CHEESE), SMALL MESH BAG (OPTIONAL), FISHING NET, A GROWN-UP (NEVER GO NEAR WATER WITHOUT ONE)

Create a paving stone gallery

YOU WILL NEED:

A FLAT HARD SURFACE SUCH AS PAVING SLABS OR TARMAC, CHALKS, PAINTBRUSH (OPTIONAL), WATER (OPTIONAL), OLD CLOTH (OPTIONAL)

Tip: If you want to restart your picture, it's easy to get a big paintbrush and some water and simply wipe away your work before letting the slab dry again.

Never underestimate the brilliance of chalk. Felt tips might be more glamorous but no one is going to yell at you for leaving the tops off your chalk. Coloured pencils may offer more colour variety but you don't have to sharpen chalk. And don't even get me started me on wax crayons. I mean, really? What's the point of them?*

Best of all, though, you can leave chalks outside. It really won't harm them. And that means they will always be to hand when you need to mark out a snail race (see page 144), set up cross step (see page 120) or even create a paving stone masterpiece.

Yes, it's easy to turn a bunch of paving slabs or even a piece of tarmac into an outdoor art gallery. Paving slabs create natural picture frames, or you can draw in your own. Then you just need to let your imagination take over.

It's good to have a few different-coloured chalks as well as some extra tools. You can use your fingers or an old cloth to smudge the chalk and create a misty effect. Also, using a slightly damp paintbrush over thick chalk can make the colour appear smoother and more solid. You can also add texture with smaller brushstrokes.

*Oh yes, that's right, nature rubbings (see page 32). My mistake. Sorry wax crayons.

Play splash

This game could just as easily be called Get Soaking Wet and Scream a Lot, but Splash makes it seem a lot less scary for the grown-ups (and neighbours).

For obvious reasons this is best played on a hot and sunny day, in swimsuits and with towels at the ready.

Begin by writing numbers one to ten on separate bits of paper and place them in a hat or container.

Next, ask a grown-up to bring out a bucket of water from which you can fill a beaker.

The 'splasher'

One child is the 'splasher' and pulls out one of the numbers at random without letting the others know what it is.

The splasher then stands in the centre of a circle with a beaker of water whilst the others take it in turns to call out a number.

When the secret number is called, the child who says it gets a surprise soaking (screaming is optional) before becoming the splasher themselves.

YOU WILL NEED:
A PEN, PAPER, HAT OR CONTAINER, BUCKET OF WATER, PLASTIC BEAKER

Tip: If you haven't got pen or paper to hand, the splasher can just think of a number from one to ten instead.

Tip: Not getting wet enough? Then try swapping the beaker for a small bucket. That should do the trick.

Sweep for bugs

Put down the vacuum cleaner – you're making the spiders nervous. We're not talking about that sort of sweeping.

Instead, this is a great way to find all sorts of fluttering bugs that can otherwise be a bit hard to spot.

First, you need to make your sweeping net. Take a wire clothes hanger (they're what you hang clothes on. Exactly – bet you've never used them for that job before) and bend the triangular middle into a circular shape. Then straighten out the hook end so you can slot it into your piece of bamboo cane before fastening it on using some strong duct tape.

You then need to attach your old pillowcase to the circular frame. You can either fold over the top edge and sew it onto the main part or just use the tape to secure it.

The best place to sweep is through some long grass on a warm day. You need to hold your net with the open end travelling first and move it through the grass in an 'S' shape as you walk slowly forward. Move the net back and forth like this eight or nine times before stopping for a few seconds to give any bees or wasps you've captured a chance to escape.

Now you can inspect your catch. Ideally, you do this by reversing your net through the coat hanger frame into a shoebox, large (empty) ice-cream tub or a similar-sized container. You can even empty it onto a white piece of card or paper. You'll be surprised by how many different bugs you can see.

To make your bug sweep net

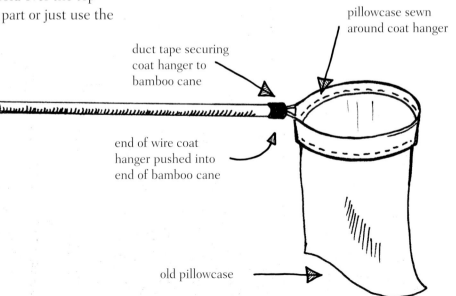

duct tape securing coat hanger to bamboo cane

pillowcase sewn around coat hanger

end of wire coat hanger pushed into end of bamboo cane

old pillowcase

YOU WILL NEED:
A WIRE CLOTHES HANGER,
BAMBOO CANE, DUCT TAPE, OLD
PALE-COLOURED PILLOWCASE,
LARGE CONTAINER OR PIECE
OF WHITE CARD OR PAPER

YOU WILL NEED:
LOGS, STUMPS OR
DRIFTWOOD, FERNS
OR OTHER WOODLAND
PLANTS, SPADE FOR
PLANTING, WOODCHIPS
(OPTIONAL), MOSS
(OPTIONAL)

Tip: If you are
building a log wall,
try driving pairs
of stakes into the
ground at intervals
and stacking the
logs between these
to prevent the wall
from collapsing.

Construct a stumpery

The Victorians invented the stumpery. Actually, the Victorians spent most of their time inventing things: steam engines, electricity, telephones, so I guess piling up a few tree stumps and giving it a fancy name was a quiet day at the office.

Still, if you want to create your own Victorian masterpiece you will simply need a few logs or lumps of woods and a nice shady spot in the garden. The idea is to arrange the 'stumps' as artfully as possible. You could pile some to create a small wall, or arrange them along the edge of a pathway.

To complete your stumpery try planting around the logs with shade-loving plants such as ferns, hostas and hellebores. You can also add moss to create a woodland feel or create a path through the stumpery using woodchips.

Best of all, your stumpery is the ideal place for many creepy crawlies to make their homes. Woodlice, millipedes and beetles will love this sort of mini garden, but just be careful not to disturb them when you go on bug hunts.

Cook with sun

Build your own oven. Learn about solar power. And bake some cookies. This is officially the Best. Science. Project. Ever.

Your shoebox will form the inner part of the oven where you cook, so you'll need to line the inside with glued-on black paper. Darker colours absorb more heat from the sun, so black is going to get the hottest of all.

Now take your bigger box, the outside of your oven, and insulate it to stop the heat escaping. You could use bubble wrap or screwed-up newspaper to do this job. You'll need to leave enough room for your shoebox to sit in the centre at the top. Now just cut the uppermost flaps of your larger box so they can be taped down to form the top of the oven, leaving only the black inside of the shoebox on show.

Use three sections of cardboard, bent lengthways, and tape them together to form three sides of a lid for the oven. Ensure they fit nice and snugly. Now cut your clear plastic or cellophane the same size as the top of the large box and tape it down along the back edge. Place your lid on top with its longest side running along the front of the box and tape the end of the two sides onto the rear of the box. Now open up your lid and tape the other three sides of the plastic to its inside, making sure to pull it tight.

Finally, to reflect as much light (and heat) as possible, cut a large section of card and cover it with aluminium foil. You can then tape this to one side of the box and use a stick to prop it into the best position. If you want to increase the light even further you can add another reflector on an adjacent side.

Now you can get cooking. Experiment with the best place to put your oven and angle your reflector before leaving it to heat for half an hour. Cut your raw cookie dough and place two or three flattened circles into the centre of the oven and quickly shut the lid. Leave until cooked (this could take two or three hours depending on how much sun you have and how airtight you've managed to make your oven).

YOU WILL NEED:

A SUNNY DAY, SHOEBOX, BLACK PAPER, GLUE, LARGER CARDBOARD BOX, ADDITIONAL CARDBOARD, BUBBLEWRAP OR NEWSPAPER, TAPE, CRAFT SCISSORS, CLEAR PLASTIC OR CELLOPHANE, ALUMINIUM FOIL, COOKIE DOUGH

To make your solar oven

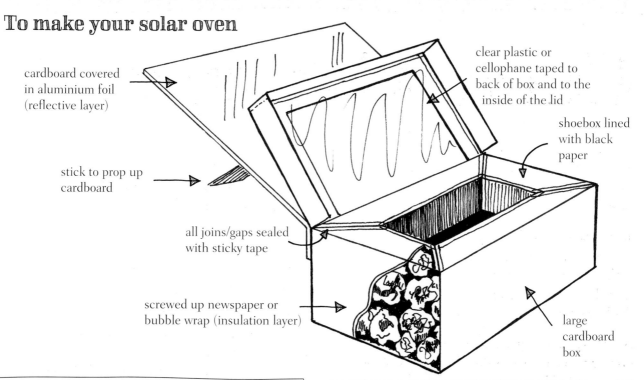

cardboard covered in aluminium foil (reflective layer)

clear plastic or cellophane taped to back of box and to the inside of the lid

shoebox lined with black paper

stick to prop up cardboard

all joins/gaps sealed with sticky tape

screwed up newspaper or bubble wrap (insulation layer)

large cardboard box

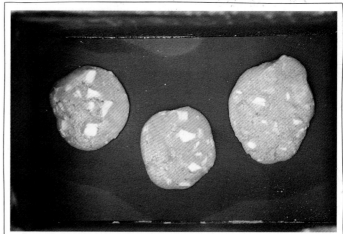

Tip: Do not skimp on your tape – making the oven as airtight as possible is key to trapping in the heat, so make sure you seal any possible gaps with the tape.

Set up camp

If you really want to spend time outdoors, camping is ideal. But you don't have to wait for your parents to book into a campsite – you can set up your own instead.

First, you're going to need to build your tent frame. This will be more stable if you can push the canes into the ground. If it's very hard and dry, try watering it well and leaving it for an hour – it will be much softer after this.

Push in two bamboo canes, leaning towards each other, and then use some twine or string to tie them together in the centre. Take the twine round and round as well as through and between the canes to make sure it's strongly bound. Do the same for the other end of the tent.

Place another cane across the top of the two triangles and again use twine to bind this together.

Finally, push a cane in from behind the tent, leaning into the top of the back triangle and tie this in – this final cane will make the structure more stable.

Throw old blankets over the top ridge of the tent and then peg them on to the canes to make the sides. Try to stretch them around the back to cover this area too, or add another blanket pegged on top to close up this gap.

Lay an old blanket on the floor inside and add cushions or bring out sleeping bags to make your tent super cosy. You could also use a solar oven (see page 90) to cook snacks, set up a washing station using old bricks, planks and a plastic bowl and even see if you can stay out late to try some stargazing (see page 184) or moth spotting (see page 152).

To make your camp

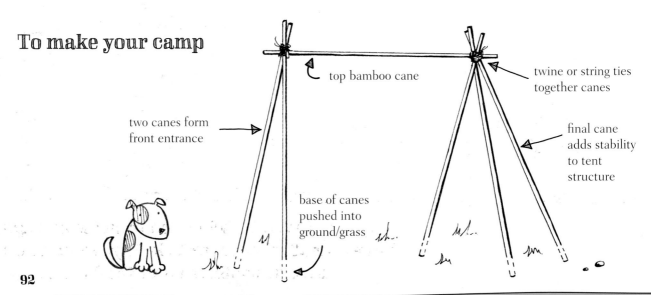

top bamboo cane

twine or string ties together canes

two canes form front entrance

final cane adds stability to tent structure

base of canes pushed into ground/grass

YOU WILL NEED:
SIX BAMBOO CANES
(1.5 OR 1.8M LONG),
TWINE OR STRING,
OLD SHEETS OR
BLANKETS, CLOTHES
PEGS, CUSHIONS OR
SLEEPING BAGS

Tip: The tent will shelter you from the odd light shower, but if you want to make it more waterproof, use a tarpaulin to cover the frame.

YOU WILL NEED:
DUCT TAPE, MASKING OR PARCEL TAPE, NATURAL OBJECTS, STICKY-BACKED PLASTIC (OPTIONAL), HOLE PUNCH (OPTIONAL), STRING OR RIBBON (OPTIONAL)

Tip: For those less keen on bracelets, you could form an arm band or belt instead.

Make a nature walk bracelet

Unless you're a dog who's been stuck in the house all day, the words 'Let's go for a walk' are unlikely to make you jump up in excitement (and hopefully you won't want to lick anyone's face either). So let's try something else. 'Who'd like to make some jewellery?' There, that's better. (Although the dog doesn't look convinced.)

First, you'll need some tape. You can use duct tape, parcel tape or masking tape. Simply wrap it around your wrist until it overlaps to form a ring – you may need to get a grown-up to help you here. Oh, and make VERY sure you do this with the sticky side on the OUTSIDE, otherwise the only bit of nature stuck to your bracelet will be every single hair on your wrist. Ouch.

Now, as you go for your walk, you can look out for natural objects with which you can decorate your bracelet. You could decide on a colour theme to match your outfit, or perhaps try to collect a rainbow of colours from red to violet.

If you want to keep your bracelet for longer you could cut it off when you get home and use sticky-backed plastic to seal in the objects. To finish, puncture with a hole at either end so you can retie it with a piece of ribbon or string to form a bracelet.

Tip: Try to cover as much of the tape as you can.

Here are some examples ...

Badger

Cat

Dog

Fox

Squirrel

Rabbit

Hedgehog

Blackbird

Tip: Why not keep a journal to record which animal prints you spotted and perhaps set up footprint traps in other parts of the garden to see if the results are different.

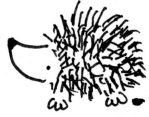
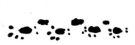

Capture animal tracks

A lot of animal visitors come out at night, which is really rather annoying – what with pesky bedtimes and the 'no walking about the garden in your PJs at midnight' rules.

But with a little detective work you can find out who's creeping around your garden at night.

You'll need to take your old baking tray and place it somewhere animals might walk. See if there are any likely looking holes in fences or place it near compost bins, or piles of leaves or logs. Now make sure the tray is laid on a nice flat piece of ground – if it wobbles, animals will be wary.

Next, wet some fine play sand with water as though you are making a sandcastle and then empty it into the tray so it fills to the top. Check the sand will show up animal prints by pressing gently on the surface and seeing if your fingers leave a mark. You can then use a long ruler to smooth it out.

To tempt creatures in, add a little saucer of bait to the middle. Dog or cat food will attract hedgehogs and foxes, or you could try some birdseed or peanuts for mice and other small mammals.

Leave the footprint trap out overnight and then check it in the morning. Use the guide opposite to try and identify any footprints you spot.

To make a sand trap

bait on saucer

damp sand levelled with ruler

old baking tray

YOU WILL NEED: OLD BAKING TRAY, PLAY SAND, WATER, RULER, SMALL DISH, BAIT (CAT OR DOG FOOD, BIRDSEED OR PEANUTS)

Play water balloon piñata

You know piñatas, right? Those things you hang up and hit until you are showered in sweets? Well, this is very similar only there are no sweets involved.

Hang on. I'm not selling this very well, am I?

OK, on the plus side you will get soaking wet and there will be balloons.

There, that's better.

First, you need to attach a rope or thick string between two posts, or tree branches, or walls – anything solid and strong. It needs to be above your head height so it's best to get a grown-up to help with this.

Now you need to fill your balloons with water. You'll need to stretch the opening of the balloon over a tap to do this and carefully fill it until its neck becomes strained. Then tie the ends and place them somewhere soft where they won't burst (a blanket on the lawn works well).

Once you've filled as many as you want to use, tie a piece of string to the neck of each and then carefully start to hang them from the rope (you may need to ask a grown-up to help with this too).

Finally, you need to find a bat. A plastic rounders or baseball bat works well, or you could use a long cardboard tube, an old broom handle cut in half or even a plastic beach spade.

Now take it in turns to try and break your piñatas. You can either have a set number of hits each or everyone can simply keep going until they burst a balloon each.

 Tip: Stand a long way back when anyone is swinging the bat or they may mistake you for a piñata.

Tip: If you want to speed things up a bit, use a bamboo pole instead and poke at the balloons rather than batting them.

YOU WILL NEED:
ROPE, BALLOONS, STRING, BAT (E.G. CARDBOARD TUBE, OLD BROOM HANDLE, ETC.)

Sign with nature

Woodland walks can sometimes get just a little bit dull. 'Look, there's a tree', 'Look, there's another tree', 'I spy something beginning with T'. 'Is it... a tree?'

You get the point.

So, to liven things up, why don't you get the family to make some trails to follow? Split into two groups with the first group going ahead. Their job is to lay down signs using only things they find lying around – twigs and stones both work well. They can clear a space on the path and create an arrow at regular intervals pointing in the direction the trackers should go.

You can also use an X sign on pathways that the trackers shouldn't take just in case they are tempted off the right path. You can even leave marks that show where secret messages are hidden, or if there are obstacles coming up.

After about ten minutes the tracking party can set off and see how long it takes them to find the trail-makers.

Next time, swap over and let the other half of the family have a go at trail-making.

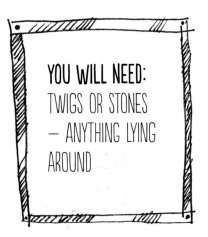

YOU WILL NEED:
TWIGS OR STONES
– ANYTHING LYING
AROUND

Some useful signs ...

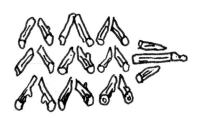

water in this direction

turn (left or right)

this way

not this way

Tip: Make sure a grown-up is with each group. It may also be good to work out a rendezvous point if the trail becomes hard to spot. Just don't say 'Let's meet by the tree'.

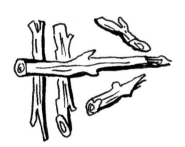

this way over obstacle

party split up

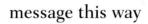

message this way

gone home

Tip: If you have any cuts or grazes, put a plaster over them before you go pond dipping and also make sure you wash your hands well after you have finished.

YOU WILL NEED:
A CONTAINER, FISHING NET, SPOON (OPTIONAL), MAGNIFYING GLASS (OPTIONAL), FIELD GUIDE (OPTIONAL), NOTEBOOK AND PENCIL (OPTIONAL) GROWN-UP (SADLY, NOT OPTIONAL)

Go pond dipping

Unfortunately, you're going to need a very large accessory for pond dipping. That's right, you'll have to take a grown-up with you. Thankfully, they can prove useful – if nothing else they can carry the rest of your equipment.

First, kneel carefully by the pond and half-fill your collecting container with some water from the pond. Now you're ready for pond dipping.

The most important thing to remember is that you are not supposed to dip yourself. To make sure this doesn't happen, stand sideways to the pond with your feet about a shoulder's width apart – this will make you more balanced and stable. Now take your fishing net and dip it into the water, then move it in a figure-of-eight pattern.

Take out your net and empty your contents into the container by turning it inside out. You can use a spoon and a magnifying glass to take a closer look at things you have caught. If you make sketches you can identify them later, or check them against a field guide there and then.

Take a look at different areas of the pond – the surface, amongst the weeds or even in the mud at the bottom. Just make sure you return all the creatures to the pond when you've finished dipping.

Hold a ball battle

Balls really should be allowed to mix more. I mean, when does a basketball ever get to hang out with a football? And have you ever seen a tennis ball invited to join a beach ball gang? Thankfully, ball battles are quite happy to welcome all comers.

First, divide your garden into two. You could use a garden hose or a long piece of rope. Now, place all the balls you can find along the length of the line.

Finally, split people into two teams and line them up an equal distance away from the line but on either side if it. On the word 'go', everyone runs to the balls and tries to throw them at the opposition. If the ball is caught, the thrower is out. If a person is hit, they are declared out. Neither team can cross the line and the first to get all the other team out is declared the winner.

Oh, and it might be best not to invite the cricket balls or golf balls to this game. There's a reason they're not allowed to play with the others. Ouch.

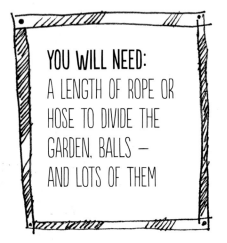

YOU WILL NEED:
A LENGTH OF ROPE OR HOSE TO DIVIDE THE GARDEN, BALLS — AND LOTS OF THEM

Eek!

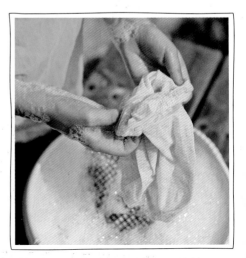

YOU WILL NEED:
BUCKETS, WATER, WASHING POWDER OR SOAP, STRING OR TWINE, POSTS (IF NOTHING SUITABLE IN GARDEN), CLOTHES PEGS, DIRTY CLOTHES

Do the laundry

Grown-ups do like a good moan, don't they? I mean, take the laundry. Anyone would think it was hard work, whereas we all know there's nothing more fun than a good washing day.

If you fancy showing those dull adults how to do it, then why not set up a garden laundry? You can volunteer to wash some of your own clothes or perhaps just spruce up your toys' outfits.

Using two plastic buckets works best – one with soapy water to wash, the other with clean water to rinse. Then you just need to roll up your sleeves and get to work.

Wring out the clothes when you are done and peg them out on a washing line. You can set this up by tying some twine or string between strong branches or posts. If you don't have either, ask a grown-up to knock two posts into the ground for you to use.

If you have a toy iron and board you can even give the clothes a smooth down when they are dry, and, for the more enterprising launderette, why not publish a price list for your clientele?

Tip: Sometimes the colour from dark clothes can run into the washing water. If this happens, make sure you change the water before washing any pale clothes in it.

Explore with an underwater viewer

Paddling in rock pools or a shallow sea is far more interesting if you can see below the surface. If you don't have goggles and a snorkel, why not create your own underwater viewer instead?

Take an empty two-litre plastic drinks bottle and remove the lid so you can squeeze it flat, then use a pair of craft scissors to cut a slit about 10cm from the bottom. Now reinflate the bottle, replace the lid and use your scissors to cut from that slit to form a rectangular opening about 20cm up the bottle and 10cm along the top and bottom. You can rub

YOU WILL NEED:
A TWO-LITRE EMPTY PLASTIC DRINKS BOTTLE, CRAFT SCISSORS, SANDPAPER (OPTIONAL), DUCT TAPE (OPTIONAL)

down the edge with sandpaper to smooth it or simply put duct tape around all the edges to cover any sharp bits.

Hold the bottle sideways and submerge the bottom section in the water. You can then look through the hole to see the wonders below. If the only 'wonders' you can see are your feet, it might be worth moving to another spot – unless your feet are particularly interesting, of course. As always, when you are near water, take a grown-up with you.

Tip: Be careful near the edge of the pond as it may be slippery.

Have a blindfold shootout

If the idea of someone shooting freezing cold water straight at you isn't nerve-wracking enough, try a blindfold shoot out to really ratchet up the tension.

You'll need four people playing – two will be shooters and two guiders. Don't worry, you can keep swapping over. After all, we wouldn't want anyone to miss out on getting soaking wet.

The two shooters are given empty water pistols, then blindfolded and a bucket of water placed about two metres from each of them. Next, the guiders turn their shooters around five times each to make sure they are a little dizzy and don't know where the bucket is.

The idea is for the guider to shout out instructions to their shooter to guide them to the bucket from where they will have to fill up their water pistol (without removing the blindfold). The guiders will then need to give the shooters instructions on which way to fire to try to hit their opponent. The first one to wet their target wins, and everyone swaps over.

YOU WILL NEED:
FOUR PLAYERS, TWO WATER PISTOLS (OR SQUEEZY BOTTLES), TWO BLINDFOLDS, TWO BUCKETS OF WATER

Tip: Lengths of material or scarves work well as blindfolds

Paint outside

Parents are really good at excuses. Don't believe me? Then just ask them this question: 'Can I paint a picture?' I almost guarantee you will hear one of the following:

'It's a lovely idea but...

...I need to set the table/clear the table/sell the table.'

...coloured pencil pictures look so much prettier.'

...I can't find the paints.'

...the dog ate the paints.'

...I sold the paints when I sold the table.'

It's almost as if they're worried you'll make a mess.

However, try this: 'Can I paint a picture...outside?' and the response will be much more positive (although less inventive).

Yes, painting outside not only reduces the chances of you spilling on something precious, it also gives you the opportunity to paint some nature-inspired masterpieces.

The most important thing to remember is it can get windy outside. Even if it doesn't seem too bad, a sudden gust can carry off pictures and knock over paint pots. If you are lucky enough to have an easel, you can use large bulldog clips or clothes pegs to attach your paper by the top and sides. If not, you can make your own with a couple of short planks or a piece of board leaning against an outdoor chair or table.

And rather than using normal paints, why not create your own from things you find outside? Use a pestle and mortar, or just a rounded stone on a tile, to crush up different materials and then add a little water so you can use the colour on your brush. Chalk stone is a great white, burnt wood or ash from a fire is black, squeezing raspberries, elderberries or rose hips through a sieve give shades of purple or red, mud is... well... mud colour, and crushed leaves and grass will be, unsurprisingly, green.

It's useful to have a low table or outdoor chair to put your paints and water on. If you want to stop things moving around and potentially falling over, you can put a large blob of sticky tack underneath. It's also worth putting over a wipeable cloth or piece of plastic to protect the surface.

YOU WILL NEED: EASEL OR BOARD AND CHAIR, TABLE, POTS, PAPER, CLIPS OR PEGS, PAINT BRUSHES, WATER, NATURAL MATERIALS, PESTLE AND MORTAR OR STONE AND TILE, WIPEABLE CLOTH (OPTIONAL), STICKY TACK (OPTIONAL)

red = raspberries,
green = grass and leaves,
black = charcoal,
white = chalk,
brown = mud

Play Arctic dress up

Let's get this straight from the start. You should only play this game in warm weather. Really warm weather. Arctic dress up is fun. Hypothermia is not.

It also requires a bit of pre-planning. The night before the game you need to gather enough T-shirts for all the contestants. Thoroughly wet them in water, then scrunch them up (or fold them) and put each in a separate plastic bag. Next, ask a grown-up to place them in the freezer overnight.

The following day, when it's nice and warm, and you're ready to play the game, take the T-shirts out of the freezer. Remove each from its bag and put one in front of every player (who should be dressed in swimsuits). On the word 'go', everyone has to try to put on their frozen T-shirt.

And here's the fun bit. Frozen scrunched-up T-shirts are not only pretty stiff and tricky to unfold, they're also...well...very cold.

Tip: If you want to increase the difficulty (and the volume of squealing) try adding frozen shorts and socks to the pile.

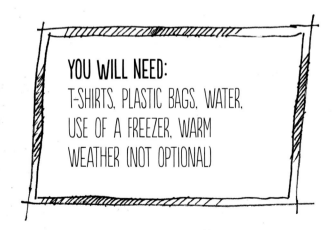

YOU WILL NEED:
T-SHIRTS, PLASTIC BAGS, WATER, USE OF A FREEZER, WARM WEATHER (NOT OPTIONAL)

YOU WILL NEED:
SAND, SPADES, TENNIS BALL
(FOR MOULDING THE RUN)

Make a sand ball run

Forget sandcastles. If you have a spade, a ball and a beach to hand, you can construct something a whole lot more exciting – a ball run.

First, you are going to need a big heap of sand. If you have something you can pile it against, that makes the job a bit easier – a large boulder, wooden groin or wall are ideal. Just make sure it won't move.

When you've made the large heap, use your hands or the back of the spade to pat it down and get rid of any soft spots. Next, start making your track.

Take the tennis ball and push it into the sand from the top, rolling it really hard and pressing down as you go so that you make a path from top to bottom. Add some gentle curves to make it more interesting.

You can also use your hands to dig out tunnels along the track. Start with one hand excavating from the top and the other from the bottom until they meet in the middle (you can even shake your own hand in congratulation). You then just keep digging out bits from the edge, top and bottom until it's big enough to get a ball through.

Perfecting the ball run is half the fun. Keep trying it from the top and add barriers of sand or dig more out until you get the ball to run from start to finish without stopping or going off the track.

Tip: If you dig down into the sand a metre or so away from the pile, you can lead the ball run into this underground area. This makes the track even longer.

Tip: You need the strength of a tennis ball to mould your run but after it's set up you can use other, lighter or softer balls to roll down it.

Build a pitfall trap

This is a great way to safely capture small animals such as insects and even amphibians and reptiles. And no, 'small animals' does not include younger brothers and sisters.

First, choose a spot that is in a quiet part of the garden where people tend not to walk. Dig a hole big enough to fit in your steep-sided container so that the top is level with the soil around it and then add a little extra soil in its base.

Space four stones around the edge of the trap and place a piece of wood or tile on top of them. This creates a roof for the pitfall trap, which stops rain getting in and also shades the trap from sun.

Leave the trap overnight and check it in the morning. You might need to look carefully in case some creatures are hiding in the soil.

Make sure you release any creatures in the trap carefully and, if you leave it in place, you must check it and release any others each morning.

YOU WILL NEED:
A SMOOTH, STEEP-SIDED CONTAINER, FOUR STONES, PIECE OF WOOD OR TILE, TROWEL, FOOD SCRAPS (OPTIONAL), FIELD GUIDES TO IDENTIFY CREATURES (OPTIONAL)

How to build a pitfall trap

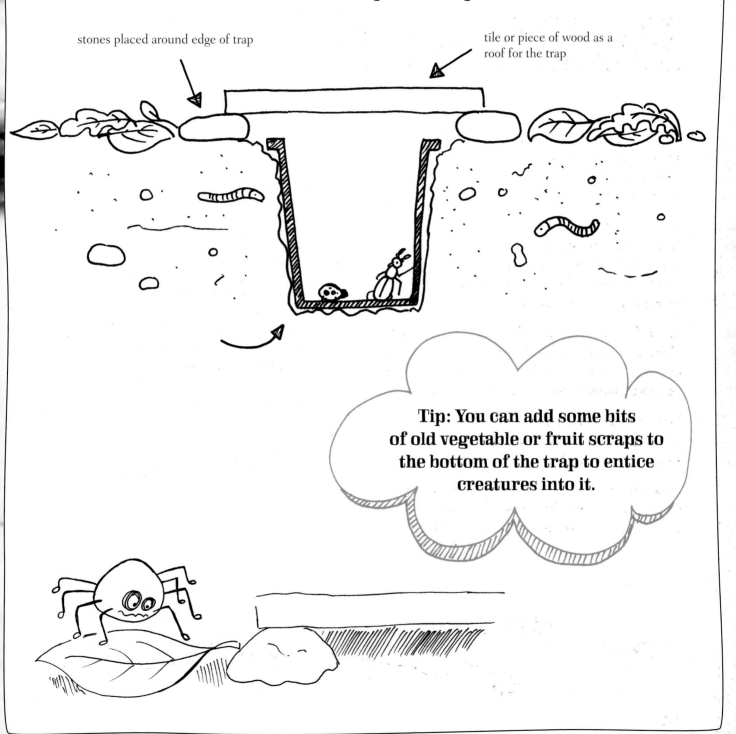

stones placed around edge of trap

tile or piece of wood as a roof for the trap

Tip: You can add some bits of old vegetable or fruit scraps to the bottom of the trap to entice creatures into it.

Tip: If you have a larger space and more time to spare, you can make the grid as large as you wish.

Play cross step

On a large patio, driveway or playground, mark out a grid with chalk, ten squares wide by ten squares long. Just make sure each square is big enough to stand in, otherwise you'll be playing 'cross tiptoe' and that's much harder work.

Next, everybody chooses a square to stand in, grabs a different colour of chalk each and the game begins. Each player takes it in turn to move to a new square either left, right, forward or back, but NOT diagonally. When they move they must put a cross in the square they were standing in before. The only rule is, you can't step into a square already crossed out.

When a player finds themselves in a 'dead end' and they can't move in any direction, they're out.

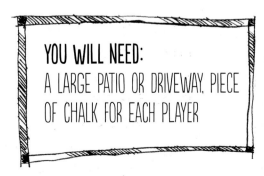

YOU WILL NEED:
A LARGE PATIO OR DRIVEWAY, PIECE OF CHALK FOR EACH PLAYER

Tip: If you only have one colour of chalk, players can write their initials in squares instead.

Make flower fairies

YOU WILL NEED:
A GARDEN, PARK OR HEDGEROW, A SMALL TWIG, INGENUITY, FASHION SENSE

You may not be aware of this, but outside your door is a very, very large wardrobe. Yes, look in your garden, local park or hedgerow and you will see tunics, hats, dresses and skirts. They may not fit you but, to a flower fairy, it's a catwalk just waiting to happen.

To construct your fairy fashionista, you'll need to start with a thin but strong twig. Now you can begin hunting for your clothes. It's a good idea to work from the middle out, so try and find a torso and arms. A ripe strawberry, which is soft enough to push some small twiggy arms into, can make a great red top, or you could try adding on a couple of ivy leaves and then threading each leaf stalk back through to form the arms.

If the twig isn't sharp enough to add holes to your leaves, flowers or seedheads before threading, you could find a separate one to make holes – or even a large thorn to do the job.

Seedheads or small fruits are ideal for heads and most gardens are filled with great flower-based hats. Foliage or large flowers make effective skirts whilst thinner, longer leaves can be perfect for trousers.

Tip: Once you've created your flower fairies, why not hunt for some more natural materials to build them a house (or a catwalk)?

Play human croquet

Tip: If you don't have enough players, you could make hoops by pushing pairs of bamboo canes into the ground.

Ever wanted to be a ball? Of course you have! Well, here's your chance.

To play human croquet you'll need quite a few players. At least two people will be blindfolded to be the 'balls'. Two other players will 'hit' them (not literally – that would be rather mean, and really take the edge off someone's long-held ambition to be a ball).

The rest of the players take the part of hoops. They spread out in pairs, arms joined in an arch and feet about a metre apart. The first ball then tucks itself into a rolling shape before being positioned by their player. When they feel they've lined them up to reach the first hoop, the player yells 'go' and their ball rolls until the player yells 'stop'. Then the next player has their turn.

The aim is to get your ball through all the hoops in the right order. Sounds easy? Well, then you've never tried rolling a blindfolded human ball – they're surprisingly tricky to manoeuvre and rarely move in straight lines. And remember – you can't yell any other instructions while they're rolling.

The winner is the first ball and player to get through the final hoop – after which the hoops take turns to swap and have a go as mallet and ball.

YOU WILL NEED:
BLINDFOLDS

Tip: A flowery wreath can also make a very effective crown.

YOU WILL NEED:
THICK GARDEN WIRE, PLANT POT, EVERGREEN FOLIAGE, DECORATIONS (E.G. FLOWERS, BERRIES, SEEDHEADS), THIN WIRE (OPTIONAL), NAIL OR HOOK (FOR GROWN-UP TO ATTACH)

Weave a wreath

A wreath is a circle of foliage or flowers which you can use to decorate doorways. Not that it matters if you make a square, rectangle or triangle instead. I mean, we wouldn't want the other shapes to feel left out, would we?

Start by taking a long length of thick garden wire. Try to use the sort which is coated in dark green plastic, as it will be easier to hide with the leaves.

If you are making a circle, wrap the wire tightly around a plant pot, twist the ends together and then wrap it around a second time and twist the ends together again. Next, take the double loop off the pot and use the rest of the wire to wrap around both the loops to make a stronger single circle. Finish the end of the wire in a hook at the top, which you can use to hang up your wreath.

The base of the wreath is best made from evergreen leaves as these will last longer. Lengths of ivy are perfect. If you have a stem of leaves, tuck one end between two pieces of wire so it's held tight, then simply wrap the rest around the frame before tucking the last piece between another two pieces of wire to secure it. Keep adding more stems until the wreath is covered.

If you don't have ivy, you can use conifer leaves instead. Here you can take a section at a time and just push or weave each stem between different sections of wire until you have covered the base.

Finally, you can add some decorations. In spring or summer this might be daisies, buttercups or other pretty flowers, in autumn it could be seed heads and in winter it might be berries. If the decorations have stems, these can be threaded into the wreath, or if there's no long stem you can attach decorations to the base with some thin garden wire.

Finally, you just need to hang your decoration somewhere. You can ask a grown-up to add a nail or hook to a doorway or a wall and use this to hook your wreath onto.

Tip: Make sure you keep weaving on leaves until all the wire is hidden.

127

Make a wind clunk

These are more traditionally called wind chimes but the sound of wood hitting wood is definitely not a chiming sound, so 'wind clunk' it is.

For the chimes – or rather clunks – you'll need some chunky sticks. Hunt around in the garden, or out on walks to find about 10 to 15 you can use. Ideally, they will be quite straight and all slightly different thicknesses and lengths as this makes for a more tuneful sound.

Tip: You can hang other natural objects, such as pinecones or conkers, from the other holes to make your clunk more interesting and add different sounds.

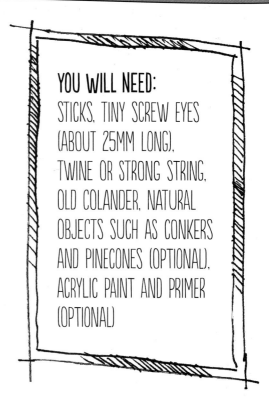

YOU WILL NEED:
STICKS, TINY SCREW EYES (ABOUT 25MM LONG), TWINE OR STRONG STRING, OLD COLANDER, NATURAL OBJECTS SUCH AS CONKERS AND PINECONES (OPTIONAL), ACRYLIC PAINT AND PRIMER (OPTIONAL)

Now take your metal eyes and screw them into the centre of one end of each stick. Push in hard to start each off and then just turn them in as far as they will go.

Thread a piece of twine or string through the eye and tie it in a knot. Now thread the other end through one of the holes in an old colander, from the inside to the outside. Finally, knot this enough times so it won't pass through the hole.

Keep doing this at regular intervals until all your sticks are dangling down from the colander when it is held upside down. Finally, thread a long length of twine through two equally spaced holes in the base of the colander and use this to hang your wind clunk from a tree branch.

Tip: To make a more colourful 'clunk' try painting your sticks with acrylic paint. If you paint them with primer first, the acrylic paint will look brighter.

Tip: If you have a dressing-up box, why not bring it outside for the costume department to rifle through?

Stage an open-air play

Why not follow Shakespeare's lead and indulge in a bit of open-air theatre this summer?

You could retell a famous fairy story. Ones with a woodland or outdoor setting work well. How about Little Red Riding Hood, Hansel and Gretel or Snow White? Better still, why not make up your own? Hey, you could even film it, sell the rights to Disney, make your fortune, move to LA... Sorry, getting a little carried away here. Where were we? Ah yes, plays.

If your garden has a naturally raised area, this would work well as a stage or you could even construct your own from old pallets with floorboards laid on top. But don't worry – it isn't really necessary.

Handily, you won't need to paint any backdrops as the garden provides these free of charge. It does add to the drama, though, if you can have some swishing stage curtains. If there is a well-placed tree branch, you could throw an old sheet over it and tie it back against the trunk when the play is in full swing. Alternatively, you could attach your sheet or old curtain to some rope or a washing line which you could suspend between any strong uprights such as fence posts or thick branches.

Finally, after creating your theatre and rehearsing the play, don't forget the audience. You can invite friends and family to bring chairs outside or simply lay down picnic rugs and cushions.

YOU WILL NEED:
OLD SHEETS OR CURTAINS, ROPE,
WASHING LINE OR HANDY BRANCH,
RUGS/CHAIRS OR CUSHIONS,
COSTUMES, YOUR IMAGINATION,
APPRECIATIVE AUDIENCE

Play beach games

A sandy beach makes a perfect outdoor games space – no hiring fees, easy to mark out, and lots and lots and LOTS of room. Plus it gets cleaned up by the sea each day ready for a rematch.

Make the most of it with some of these games:

Frisbee golf

Make your 'holes' by marking the tee (from where you start throwing the frisbee) and the hole (a circle drawn on the sand – bigger circles are good for younger or less 'practised' frisbee throwers). If you are throwing quite a long distance, it's worth adding a marker for your 'hole' – perhaps a stone tower (see page 190) – so it's easier to see.

YOU WILL NEED: A BEACH, FRISBEES (FOR FRISBEE GOLF), A BUCKET AND SMALL CUP OR BEAKER PER TEAM (FOR SEAWATER DASH)

Giant noughts and crosses

Draw an open 3 x 3 grid on the sand, as large as you like. One person starts by adding a cross (X) to one box, the second player adds a nought (O) – keep going until one has three in a row (across, down or diagonally) – but the trick is to make sure you block the other player before they manage it first. Swap over who goes first each time.

If you want more of a challenge, play giant 'Connect Four' on a grid 7 across by 6 up. In this game you have to start from the bottom up and, after the first row, you can only add your X or O on top of one already there. The first to make four in a row, wins.

Beach cross step

Draw a 10 x 10 grid on the sand and then follow the instructions on page 120 but instead of using coloured chalk crosses, write your initials OR use different-coloured stones or types of shells for each separate player to mark their squares.

Jellyfish

Draw a wiggly shape on the sand – this is your jellyfish. Now all stand round it holding hands in a circle. On the word 'go', without letting go of each other's hands, everyone has to try to pull fellow players towards the jellyfish – anyone stepping on it will be 'stung' and out of the game. You can keep going until there is only one survivor who is then declared the winner.

Seawater dash

Two teams or more have a large bucket each and a small cup or beaker. Everyone starts behind a line about 10 or 20 metres from the sea. On 'go', the first players in each team race to the sea, fill their cup and race back to add it to the bucket. The next person then goes and so on. The winning team is the one to fill their bucket first but, beware, speed and spillages often go together.

Tip: Mud pies are NOT edible (just in case you were wondering).

Build a mud pie kitchen

Tip: If you want to add a restaurant feel to your mud pie creation, why not get an outdoor blackboard or slate tile to write up 'Today's Specials'?

YOU WILL NEED:
OLD CRATES OR BRICKS, OLD PLANKS, PLASTIC OR STAINLESS STEEL BOWLS AND CONTAINERS, WOODEN OR PLASTIC SPOONS, NATURAL INGREDIENTS

Let's get this clear from the start. This is about making a mud pie kitchen, not making mud pies in a kitchen. The first will cause your parents to smile with pride at your creativity, the second will involve them screaming 'what have you DONE?' before grounding you for the next ten years.

So first of all, leave the kitchen. In fact, leave the house. Next, find a place to create your mud pie kitchen outside. You had better double check this with parents first if you don't want to encounter the whole screaming/grounding thing again.

You will need to set up a work surface. Old wooden or plastic crates are good for this, or stacks of bricks bridged by old planks. If you can add the odd shelf somewhere, then even better – it will give you somewhere to store your utensils and ingredients.

Try to find some containers and old kitchen equipment for mixing your pies. Plastic washing up bowls and jugs, stainless-steel dishes and plastic or wooden spoons all work well as they won't break easily and can be left outside.

Then it's about collecting ingredients. Obviously, mud or dirt is top of the list, but feel free to add sand, leaves, grass, twigs and, well, pretty much anything really. And don't forget water – just to make sure everything sticks together in a gloopy, yucky mess.

Make a weather vane

YOU WILL NEED:

A PLANT POT, ACRYLIC PENS OR EXTERIOR PAINT, SOIL, STRAW, PENCIL (WITH RUBBER END), PIN, BEAD, THICK PIECE OF PLASTIC, STRONG TAPE (E.G. DUCT TAPE), COMPASS, GRAVEL OR STONES (OPTIONAL)

Knowing which way the wind is blowing can be very useful, particularly if you're doing an impression of a pirate captain ('Ooo Arrrr, there be a strong north-easterly this morning'), or if you're next to someone who's had baked beans for lunch and you don't want to be caught downwind.

Thankfully, it is very easy to make your own weather vane, which will help you through these tricky situations.

First, take a plant pot and some outdoor paint or acrylic paint pens and write the compass points at equal distances around the side – N for North, E for East, S for South and W for West. Next, fill the pot with soil, firming it down hard as you go.

Then cut a triangular arrow point and a larger tail end shape out of some plastic (milk cartons or old food trays work well for this) before taping these to either end of your straw. Now place your straw along your outstretched finger and move it until it's in balance. This is the point where you need to push a pin right through the straw, then through a bead and finally into the rubber end of a pencil. Finally, push the nib end of the pencil into the centre of the pot.

Now you just need to use a compass so you can line up the direction signs on your pot and you're ready to read the direction of the wind (preferably not one made by eating baked beans).

Tip: You can dress the surface of the soil with gravel to make it look a little smarter.

Play water balloon toss

The idea of this game is NOT to burst the water balloon. I know: weird idea, isn't it?

First fill up and tie your water balloons and place them carefully on a soft blanket or towel outside until you're ready to use them.

Next, everyone pairs up and then stands in a line facing their partners. One person from each pair is given a water balloon and must gently throw it to their partner who will try to catch it without it bursting.

After each successful catch, the thrower takes a step back, making the next throw a little bit trickier. The winners are the pair who manage to keep their balloon intact over the longest distance.

YOU WILL NEED:
WATER BALLOONS (OR EGGS)

Tip: For an even messier version, try playing the game with raw eggs!

Trail ants

They have no ears, fight to the death and can lift 20 times their own bodyweight. It's a fact: ants are interesting.

If you want to find out how clever they are, why not look around outside and see if you can find some? When you've spotted a group, watch what they are doing. Ants are team players, so you'll probably notice them working together – and often following each other in a line. This is because they leave a scent trail of something called 'pheromones' to guide other ants to a new home or to a source of food.

If you want to see this in action, try placing a small piece of paper along an ant trail. See what happens. Are they confused? How long does it take before they reinstate their trail over the paper? And then, what happens if you turn the paper around?

Or why not see how long it takes them to find a new source of food? Try leaving a slice of apple or a piece of banana a little way from the trail. Check back every half an hour and see how long it takes them to find it. Also, you can put the food inside an enclosure which you can make

YOU WILL NEED:
ANTS, PAPER, SMALL
BITS OF FOOD

just by placing some sticks around it on the ground. Once the 'treat' has been discovered and a new trail formed, take away the sticks (which will be part of the scent trail) and see what happens.

You could even have a go at being an ant yourself. Try working in a team with your brothers/sisters/friends and have a go at lifting 20 times your bodyweight. Actually, come to think of it, this is never going to work. Just watch the experts instead.

Warning: Ants can bite, so be careful not to pick any up or get too close.

Ants are great weightlifters

Tip: Many diaries and calendars will tell you when to expect a full moon.

Create a moonlight garden

YOU WILL NEED:
WHITE STONES, SHELLS OR PEBBLES, NIGHT-SCENTED OR PALE/WHITE-FLOWERED PLANTS, PALE OR WHITE POTS (WHITE PAINT AND BRUSH), SOLAR-POWERED FAIRY LIGHTS (OPTIONAL), TEA LIGHTS AND JARS

Nights are dark, right? Well, actually, not always. In fact, moonlight can be very light. The clue is in the name. So how about creating a moonlight garden to make the most of it?

First, you need to find out when there is a full moon as this will offer the most light. Then you can spend the day preparing your magical garden. Use white stones or shells to mark out a pathway and seating area. If you place these on a lawn or dark earth they will show up best.

Now you need to add some plants. If you have any pale-coloured pots these work well, or you could even recoat old terracotta pots with white paint to make them glow in the moonlight. If you start planning this early in the year you could even have sown the pots with some night-scented stock (*Matthiola longipetala*) or sweet rocket (*Hesperis matronalis*) seeds. When these plants have grown they smell fantastic in the evening, making them perfect for your night garden. Another great night-scented plant is honeysuckle, so if you have one of these climbers in your garden it's worth creating your magical spot as near to it as you can.

If you don't have either, just choose some lovely white plants – these show up brilliantly in moonlight.

Finally, if you want to add some magic starlight, you could thread some solar-powered fairy lights through your plants and let them twinkle when the sun goes down. Or you can place tea lights in old jam jars and use these to line the path (ask a grown-up to light them).

Dew falls in the evening, which can make it quite damp on the ground, so it's best to take out some old blankets to lie on. And there you have it – a moonlight garden, perfect for stargazing (see page 184) and consuming midnight feasts.

Hold a snail race

YOU WILL NEED:
CHALK, SNAILS, STICKERS, WINNERS' PODIUM AND TROPHIES (OPTIONAL, BUT YOU DON'T WANT TO DISAPPOINT THE SNAILS)

OK, so 'racing' might be pushing it, but I'd like to see you do better with one slime-covered foot and a house on your back. Yeah. Doesn't sound so easy now, does it?

If you want to see a bunch of gastropods galloping, you'll first need to set up your racetrack. Find a smooth surface, preferably in the shade – snails aren't fans of the sun. Next, draw on two rings with chalk – a small inner ring about 10–20cm across, the outer much larger.

Tip: Pick up your snail very gently as their shells are delicate, and always remember to return them to where they were found.

Now you will need to hunt for competitors. Try to look in damp and shady places, such as inside old plant pots, within hedges or on the undersides of large leaves. Pick them up gently and place a sticker on their shells – a different colour or number for each team.

On starter's orders, the snails should be placed behind the line of the inner circle facing outwards. The winner will be the one who crosses the outer circle line first.

Do feel free to tempt your snail with tasty leaves and treats, but a word of warning – shouting might not have much effect. Have you seen ears on a snail? Exactly.

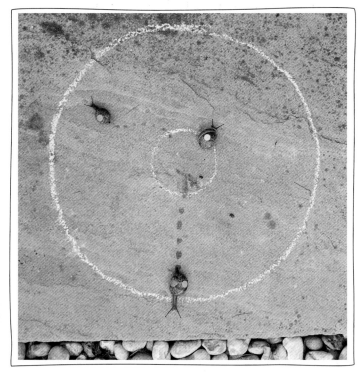

Make a mini wildlife pond

YOU WILL NEED:

A PLASTIC STORAGE BOX (AT LEAST 45 LITRES), STICK OR SAND FOR MARKING, SPADE, SAND, BRICKS AND STONES, PEBBLES, RAINWATER, NATIVE PONDWEED

Tip: In winter, leave a tennis ball floating on top of the pond – it should stop the pond freezing over completely, which would kill the wildlife inside.

As much fun as it would be to have a moat with a drawbridge or a fishing lake, most gardens are a little small for such water features. Thankfully, even a mini pond can attract some very interesting wildlife visitors and it's a lot quicker to make.

First, take your plastic storage box and place it upside down on the ground so you can mark out the size of the hole with a stick or by trickling around some pale coloured sand. Then get digging. You can place the soil to one side – it could even make a nice mounded area next to the pond which you could plant up.

Dig a little deeper than you need and then make sure you take out any sharp stones you see. Add a layer of sand to the bottom of the hole so that the top of the plastic box sits level with the surrounding soil when it is placed in the hole. You then need to backfill around the container to fill any gaps.

Place bricks and stones, or even tiles, on one side in the 'pond' to give creatures a way to get in and out. If the bricks have holes in them, these provide useful places for creatures to hide.

You can also use pieces of stone around the top of the pond to disguise the plastic edges of the storage box.

Finally, put some pebbles on the bottom, add rainwater and some pondweed. Now all you need to do is wait and see which visitors come to check out your new water feature.

Tip: keep your pond clear of rubbish such as fallen leaves and flowers, as these can rot down and make the water very smelly.

To make your wildlife pond ...

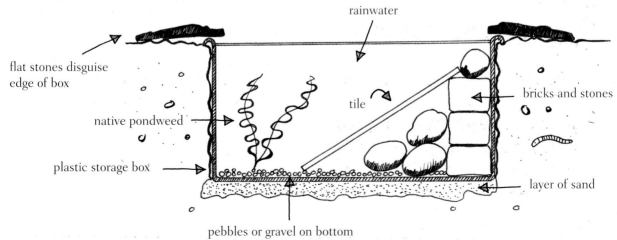

rainwater

flat stones disguise
edge of box

native pondweed

plastic storage box

tile

bricks and stones

layer of sand

pebbles or gravel on bottom

YOU WILL NEED:
A CLEAR PLASTIC FOOD POT WITH LID, PLASTICINE, BALLPOINT PEN, WIDE DRINKING STRAWS (AT LEAST 6MM ACROSS), GAUZE OR OLD TIGHTS

Tip: You can add a green sticker to the 'sucking-in straw' and a red one to the 'insect-collecting straw' so you don't get confused.

Use a pooter

'I know an old woman who swallowed a fly, I don't know why she swallowed a fly, perhaps she'll die.'

Actually, I do know why she swallowed a fly. She didn't use a pooter. A ridiculous name, yes, but very useful for collecting small insects, without accidentally swallowing them.

To make your own pooter, take a small, clear plastic food container with a lid and make sure it's thoroughly washed (small insects landing in blobs of hummus isn't a good idea).

Now take the bottom section and place it on its side on top of a large lump of plasticine before pushing a ballpoint pen through the plastic and into the plasticine to create a hole. Keep pushing the pen until your hole is big enough to fit in the straw. Now add another hole in the opposite side using the same method.

Cut your straw in half and then take one piece and cut off a 2cm section. Next, make a 2cm slit down one side of the rest of the straw before pushing this through one of the holes. Now place your gauze or piece of old tights over the slit end, before pushing the 2cm section of straw over both from inside the pot. This forms part of the straw you will suck through and the gauze will stop you swallowing any critters by accident.

Push the second half of the straw into the other hole, replace the lid and you're ready to go.

Take your pooter outside and, when you find a small creature you want to study more closely, place the collection straw close to it and then quickly suck hard on the other straw. This creates a vacuum in the container, pulling in the insect. To release it back, take off the lid and carefully tip up the pot so it can escape.

To make your pooter...

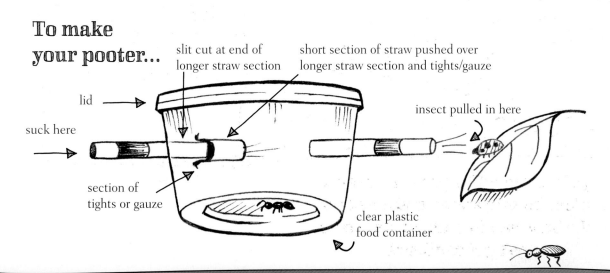

slit cut at end of longer straw section

short section of straw pushed over longer straw section and tights/gauze

lid

suck here

insect pulled in here

section of tights or gauze

clear plastic food container

Hold your own flower and produce show

Late summer, when vegetables have grown and gardens are blooming, is the perfect season for local flower and produce shows or country fairs. It's time for everyone to show off their giant turnips, perfect dahlias and homemade jams.

If you don't have a local show to enter, don't worry – you can get together with your friends or family to hold your own.

First, you'll need to decide which categories you'll have. Try to work out what your friends will be able to bring along and don't forget that shows often have an art and craft category.

Here are some ideas:

Weirdest-shaped vegetable
Tastiest cake
Longest carrot
Most colourful salad
Garden collage
Miniature garden
Flower arrangement in a teacup
Smallest tomato

You'll need to set up a table or two outside to display all the entries. And don't forget to make some certificates for first, second and third places – you can even leave a space for 'judge's comments'.

If you want to enter yourself, you might want to ask a grown-up to judge all the entries. And while you're at it, why not drop some hints about 'prizes being a nice idea'?

Tip: Why not make some paper rosettes for the winners?

YOU WILL NEED:
TABLES FOR DISPLAYING ENTRIES, CERTIFICATES, PRIZES (OPTIONAL)

Spot moths

Moths might not always be as colourful as butterflies, but you get to stay up until it's dark to spot them, which makes them much cooler.

First, grab your white sheet and pin it to a washing line or hang it over a branch. Then take a large torch and shine it at the sheet. Your hand will get very tired holding it all the time, so prop it up with some bricks or stones to give yourself an easier job.

Now you need to sit and wait. It shouldn't be long before moths start to land on the sheet and you can use a field guide to see how many different ones you can identify.

If grown-ups tell you it's late and time to go to bed, try saying 'But, dear parent, I'm just waiting to see if I can spot a Lesser Broad-bordered Yellow Underwing before I turn in.' That should leave them so speechless you'll get at least another ten minutes.

YOU WILL NEED:
A WHITE SHEET, WASHING LINE OR A BRANCH, PEGS, LARGE POWERFUL TORCH, FIELD GUIDE FOR IDENTIFYING MOTHS, STONES OR BRICKS, SMALLER TORCH (FOR READING FIELD GUIDE)

Create autumn leaf art

YOU WILL NEED:
LEAVES AND A CREATIVE IMAGINATION

Tip: You could use other autumn finds such as conkers or berries to add details to your artwork.

If you've ever left the top off a glue stick or felt-tip pen, then you will know that art supplies don't come cheap. Or at least this is what you will have been told by a grumpy grown-up, possibly accompanied with some serious frowning and the phrase 'money doesn't grow on trees, you know'.

Thankfully, outdoor art supplies do grow on trees. Yes, come autumn, you can leave your sticking and cutting to one side and get creative with a seemingly endless supply of autumn leaves.

Parks are a great place to go, as they often have a large variety of trees and this means loads of different colours – from yellows, pinks and oranges to browns and reds. They'll also be in all sorts of shapes and sizes.

You could make a fiery dragon, some exploding fireworks, or perhaps create a winding path of leaves, with colours changing as it goes along.

Even if you only have one type of leaf, you can use these to spell out your name or a special message on your lawn.

There is no end to the possibilities, and best of all, not a glue stick or grumpy adult in sight.

Tip: Why not create a beautiful butterfly, and become part of the picture.

Tip: If you can't wait for spring to see your flowers, you can always draw some on the outside of your bucket with acrylic paint pens.

To make your bulb bucket ...

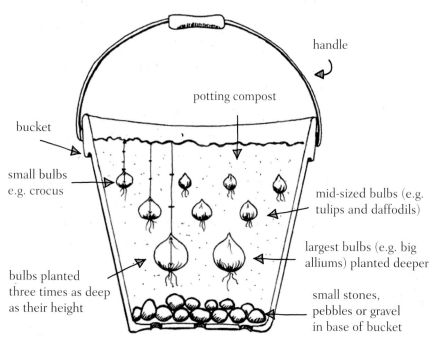

handle

potting compost

bucket

small bulbs e.g. crocus

mid-sized bulbs (e.g. tulips and daffodils)

largest bulbs (e.g. big alliums) planted deeper

bulbs planted three times as deep as their height

small stones, pebbles or gravel in base of bucket

Plant a bulb bucket

'There's a hole in my bucket, dear Liza, dear Liza, there's a hole in my bucket, dear Liza a hole.'

'Well plant it, dear Henry. And please stop repeating yourself.'

OK, so the original song might have been slightly different, but this version makes a lot more sense.

If you have a bucket with a hole or a slit, don't worry. It might not be great at carrying water, but it's perfect for planting bulbs in the autumn. In fact, you might have to ask a grown-up to make you a few more holes (with a drill for plastic or a hammer and nail for metal). This will stop the compost getting too soggy because plants need to have air in the soil as well as water.

Next, fill the bottom of the bucket with a shallow layer of small stones, pebbles or gravel (this stops the holes getting bunged up) and then add your potting compost, firming it down as you go.

You can use different types of bulbs in a single bucket, just remember to leave some space between them and plant each bulb to the depth of three times its height.

You can even have more than one layer of bulbs. For example, large alliums followed by hyacinths, small daffodils and then a crocus at the top.

Make sure you keep your bucket well watered if there hasn't been much rain. You can check if it needs watering by pushing your finger in about 3cm. If the soil is dry there, it needs a drink.

YOU WILL NEED:
AN OLD BUCKET, SMALL STONES, PEBBLES OR GRAVEL, POTTING COMPOST, VARIETY OF BULBS, ACRYLIC PAINT PENS (OPTIONAL)

Fly a homemade kite

YOU WILL NEED:
A SQUARE OF PAPER (ABOUT 25 X 25CM), TAPE, HOLE PUNCH, STRING, TOILET ROLL INNER, RIBBON

A homemade kite sounds a wonderful idea, doesn't it? Well, until you realise you're going to have to find sheets of plastic, carefully measure out templates, saw wooden dowels, bind and glue them together, tape everything carefully to the frame, all while standing on one leg and hopping backwards. OK, I made that last bit up, but you get the idea. Homemade kites can be a little bit complicated. In fact, by the time you've made it the wind will probably have died down.

So try this version instead. Five folds, three holes, a bit of tape, four knots and you're away. Yes, that's right, it's the five-minute kite.

First, take your square of paper and fold one corner over to the one diagonally opposite, then press down the fold to form a triangle. Now bend back one of these corners so its side lines up perfectly to the middle fold and press it flat. Do this again for the other side. It should now be looking a bit like a paper aeroplane.

Take the free corner of the smaller triangle and bend this backwards so it lines up perfectly with the second fold. Do the same with the other side.

Add some tape to the base of the ridge (middle fold) line as well as the top inside corner of the smallest triangle – this will help strengthen and reinforce these areas. Finally, puncture all three of these taped areas using a hole punch.

To make your kite ...

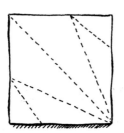
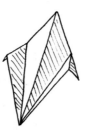
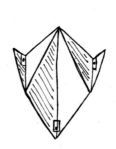
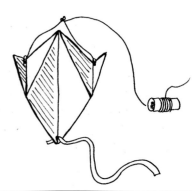

Cut two 20cm-long pieces of string and tie each to the two midway holes before tying the pieces to each other in the middle. Now attach a long piece of string (about 7–8m) to this middle knot and tie the other end to your toilet roll inner before wrapping it around to form your reel.

Finally, attach some ribbon to the bottom hole to act as a tail.

And that's it. Now all that's left is to run around outside and launch your kite. You can let out different amounts of string from your reel depending on the wind and how high you want to fly the kite.

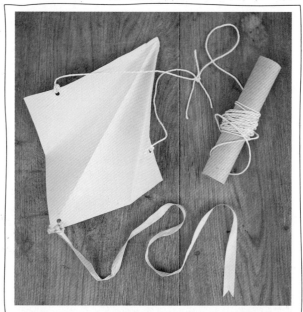

YOU WILL NEED:
AN OLD TEA TOWEL (OR SOMETHING
TO COVER THE TREASURES), TRAY
(OPTIONAL)

Tip: Some berries can be poisonous so always wash your hands after picking them up. If you're a young child, make sure you have a grown-up with you when looking for autumn treasures.

Play the autumn treasure memory game

Autumn is a generous season. Like a thoughtful aunt, it's always giving you gifts. One minute it's fresh apples and blackberries, the next it's pinecones and conkers.

So when you're in the garden or out on a walk, try picking up as many different autumn 'gifts' as you can – different-coloured leaves, fruit, seedheads, nuts. You can even hold a competition to see who can find the largest variety.

When you've gathered together your treasures (around 15 to 20 works well) why not play the memory game?

Lay out everything on an outdoor table, tray or a clear space on the ground. Everyone has a minute to remember all they can before the whole lot is covered (you can use an old tea towel for this, or, if you're out on a walk, why not just use someone's jacket?).

The person holding the cloth then removes an item without the others seeing, before revealing the treasures again. The first person to spot what's missing wins – and then it's their turn to cover everything up and remove another treasure.

Watch worms work

Believe it or not, worms are useful for more than just causing people to go 'Ewww'. They make soil healthier and turn things like old leaves and leftovers into perfect plant food. So maybe it's time you stopped dangling that poor worm in front of your sister's face and learnt a bit more about how they work.

Take your old plastic bottle and carefully cut off the top section – if this leaves a very sharp edge, you can cover it with some duct tape. Next, add a 5cm layer of moist soil to the bottom, followed by a 5cm layer of sand, then another of soil, and then sand and so on before finishing with a few old food scraps like vegetables or overripe fruit. You should also leave about a 5cm gap at the top.

Now you can go and hunt for worms. They like to be somewhere dark and damp so you'll find them burrowing in soil. If you're struggling to find any, wait until it's been raining hard and try again – worms need air to breathe so will burrow upwards if the soil is full of water. If there's no rain, you can get the same effect by soaking some soil with a hose and waiting half an hour for the worms to rise.

Pop some worms in your worm tower and cover over the top using clingfilm with several small holes poked in it (so the worms have air) and secure this with an elastic band or two. Now get a dark plastic bag and cut out a section large enough to wrap around the bottle with a little space at the end which you can secure in place with clothes pegs. This will keep out the light (which worms don't like). Place it somewhere dark and cool (but not freezing cold) and let the worms get to work.

Keep checking on progress every couple of days and see how the worms are doing. Have they mixed up the layers? Have they eaten the scraps?

If you want to see how different worms work, you can set up another wormery, this time using brandling or tiger worms. These are the red worms you can find in compost heaps. Have a race between the two sets of worms to see which work the fastest and which digest the food scraps first.

When the worms have thoroughly mixed up the soil and sand and digested the food, you can put the magic mixture on your garden and let the worms find some new work to do.

YOU WILL NEED: 2-LITRE PLASTIC BOTTLE, SCISSORS, DUCT TAPE (OPTIONAL), SOIL, SAND, WATER, FOOD SCRAPS, ELASTIC BANDS, CLINGFILM, BLACK PLASTIC BAG, CLOTHES PEGS, WORMS

Tip: Don't let the soil dry out.
It should be damp (but not wet)
as worms breathe through their
skins, which have to be moist.

Blow giant bubbles

YOU WILL NEED: TWO 1M-LONG BAMBOO CANES OR DOWELS, STRING, SCISSORS, WASHING-UP LIQUID, WATER, GLYCERINE (OPTIONAL)

It's a simple mathematical equation: if blowing bubbles is good fun, blowing giant bubbles must be enormous fun.

Here's how you do it. First, take your two pieces of dowel or bamboo cane. Then cut a piece of string, just longer than the length of the cane, and tie the ends to the top of both poles, about 2cm in. Now take a piece about half this length and tie the ends to the bottom of each pole, again about 2cm from the end. This bottom string will help stop you pulling the canes too widely apart.

Finally, cut a piece of string just over twice as long as one of the poles and tie it to either end of the top string, a centimetre in from each pole.

Now it's time to make your bubble mix. The simplest way is to mix ½ cup of washing-up liquid with 1½ cups of water and mix them thoroughly.

You can put this concoction in a shallow container before dipping the string in so it can absorb some of the mixture. When you take it out, gently pull apart the canes and you should see a bubble start to form in the triangle of the string. If there's no wind to blow your bubble, walk along to make the bubble form.

Tip: You can use some strong duct tape to stop the string slipping off the poles, or else ask a grown-up to cut some notches into the poles onto which you can tie the string.

Tip: To make a stronger bubble mix, ask a grown-up to buy some glycerine from a chemist or cake shop. Add a few drops to the mixture and leave overnight.

Play torch tag

As if it wasn't exciting enough to still be up when it's dark, you can add to the excitement with a game of torch tag.

The one chosen as 'it' has a flag or something similar to guard, and, most importantly, a torch to hold. The other players spread out around the area and then have to move as quietly as possible towards the flag, using bushes and trees to cover their movements.

'It' can move about, but their job is to guard the flag. If they hear anyone they can turn on the torch to 'tag' them by shining it on them – and, if successful, that person is 'out'. They can either stand still where they are, or go to a 'jail' area.

The player who captures the flag wins – or if no one manages the task, then the last person left in is declared the winner and becomes 'it'.

Remember, the person with the torch cannot simply spin round and round with it switched on permanently. This is not what we call playing night-time tag – it is impersonating a lighthouse, and the two are very different things.

SAFETY: When playing out at night, check where you are allowed to roam and make sure you are always well away from busy roads and traffic. It's worth having a regular headcount to make sure everyone's there, and younger children should team up with someone older so they're never wandering on their own.

YOU WILL NEED:
THREE OR MORE PEOPLE, TORCH, FLAG (OR SIMILAR OBJECT TO GUARD)

Collect flower seeds

YOU WILL NEED:
PLAIN ENVELOPES, PENS AND
COLOURED PENCILS TO DECORATE
WITH, PLANTS TO COLLECT FROM,
PAPER BAGS

Tip: Be careful – some plant seeds are poisonous if eaten (although not those listed here). However, to be safe, always follow these two golden rules – never put any in your mouth and always wash your hands after handling seeds.

You know when parents say 'I much prefer homemade presents'? Well, sometimes they really mean it. Not necessarily when you've built them a life-size replica of the Death Star from old loo roll inners, but most of the time it's true.

So how about a thoughtful homemade gift from the garden? Not only will they give you the smile that says 'you'll be getting extra ice cream for pudding', it also saves your pocket money.

You can create homemade seed packets from plain envelopes you've decorated. Make sure you have included the name of the flower and some growing instructions (you may need to ask a grown-up for help on this one – although not the one you're giving it to, obviously).

Some of the best seeds to collect are from annual plants. Because they only live for a year, they have lots of seeds they want to scatter. If you have plants like cornflowers (*Centaurea cyanus*), pot marigolds (*Calendula officinalis*), poached egg plant (*Limnanthes douglasii*) and nasturiums, just leave the old flowers on after they have finished blooming and wait until the seeds are ready to be released.

The easiest way to check is by putting a paper bag over the seedhead and then shaking it inside the bag – if it releases its seeds, they're ready for collecting.

Next, cut off the seed heads into a labelled paper bag (use a different one for each type), and then, when you've finished all your collecting, carefully put the seeds into the correct packets.

Make autumn crowns

Obviously, the world would be a better place if you were in charge, so perhaps it's time for a coronation. Thankfully, autumn abounds with plenty of crown-making material to construct your own headpiece.

First, take a long strip of card (you may need to join two together to have enough length). Staple or tape it so it will fit around your head and then put a thick piece of double-sided sticky tape all around the outer surface.

You can then go outside and begin making your crown by attaching leaves to it, carefully pulling back the sticky tape backing as you need it.

If you are out and about with no card, you can make your own crown base. You will need some very bendy twigs – young, slender, new growth works well. If you plait three lengths, about 50cm long, you can then bend this into a circular shape and weave the ends into each other to stop it unravelling. Then add a few more lengths, woven in and out, to strengthen the structure.

You can decorate your crown with leaves by slipping the leaf stalks between the twigs, which will hold them firm.

YOU WILL NEED:
CARD, DOUBLE-SIDED STICKY TAPE, STAPLER OR STRONG TAPE, TWIGS, LEAVES

 Tip: Why not add some seedheads or berries to your crown for extra adornment?

Tip: Overlap the leaves slightly to cover up more of the card.

Play sevensies

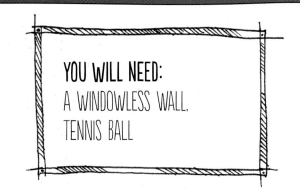

YOU WILL NEED:
A WINDOWLESS WALL,
TENNIS BALL

If you want to make a grown-up nervous, simply stand in your house with a tennis ball in one hand and a look of boredom on your face. Within seconds, most adults will not be able to help themselves uttering a desperate cry of 'Don't you DARE throw that ball inside!'

Of course, you were never going to, because there is a whole lot more fun to be had outside. Especially playing sevensies.

This is something you can practise on your own or play with friends. Ideally, you need a hard, flat surface next to a smooth wall (preferably free of windows – or else we'll have nervous grown-ups again).

The aim is to complete a series of throws and bounces – starting with a relatively simple one seven times, a slightly trickier one six times, and so on, until you're doing one very complicated throw. Once you've completed them all, you work your way backwards until you're back up to the seven again.

Throw the ball against the wall, let it bounce and catch it (seven times).

Throw the ball against the wall and catch (six times).

Throw the ball so it hits the floor, then the wall, and catch (five times).

Throw the ball under your leg so it hits the wall, then catch (four times).

Bounce the ball on the ground and use your palm to bat it against the wall then catch (three times).

Throw the ball against the wall and catch with one arm behind your back (twice).

Throw the ball against the wall, turn a full circle and catch (once).

If you're playing with others, you have to drop out and pass on the ball whenever you fail to complete a set of tasks. Next time you have to start at this same point again.

Make a rain gauge

YOU WILL NEED:
A PLASTIC DRINKS BOTTLE, CRAFT SCISSORS, STONES, PERMANENT MARKER, RULER, TAPE

It's raining cats and dogs/chucking it down/ drizzling a bit. All these descriptions might be colourful, but they're hardly accurate. I mean, exactly how many cats and dogs are we talking about?

If you want a bit more precision in your rain measurement, it's time to set up a rain gauge.

Take an old plastic soft drinks bottle without the lid – two-litre ones are a good size – and carefully cut off the top third with a pair of craft scissors (you might need a grown-up to help you). Place some stones in the bottom (this will stop it blowing over) and then fill with water until these are covered and carefully mark this point with your pen. Using a ruler, mark up from there in centimetres and, if you can, millimetres (or at least 5mm) to make a scale.

Finally, turn the cut-off top of the bottle upside down, place it inside the bottom part and tape it in place. Your rain gauge now needs to be placed outside somewhere in the open where it's not under any overhanging trees, shrubs or buildings.

Check the rain gauge every day at the same time and see if the levels have risen. Record this before emptying the water and refilling to the base level again.

Best of all, when someone declares it's raining 'cats and dogs', you can say: 'Well, we did experience 12mm of precipitation overnight but I definitely didn't record any falling animals.'

To make your rain gauge...

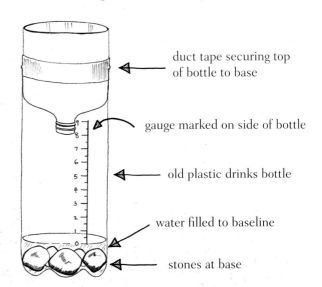

duct tape securing top of bottle to base

gauge marked on side of bottle

old plastic drinks bottle

water filled to baseline

stones at base

Create your own nature exhibit

How about impressing everyone with your budding natural scientist skills by creating a mini exhibition?

First, you'll need to get together your explorer kit. You can probably do without the tent or pith helmet, but it could prove useful to have a few bags or pots for putting your specimens in, as well as a magnifying glass to take a closer look at them and a notebook to scribble down where you found your various discoveries.

When you have finished gathering your outdoor treasures, you can use trays, or even make your own divided specimen box to display them in your exhibition.

You could try finding different rocks and stones and see if you can identify each type.

Or make a collection of seeds and nuts and write down what each will grow into.

At the seaside, why not amass a collection of shells and research which creatures used to live in each?

In fact, you can create all sorts of different displays. One word of advice, though: an 'animal droppings' exhibit may not be a great idea.

How to make your own specimen box...

YOU WILL NEED:
COLLECTING BAGS,
MAGNIFYING GLASS
(OPTIONAL), NOTEBOOK
(OPTIONAL), DISPLAY
BOX OR TRAY

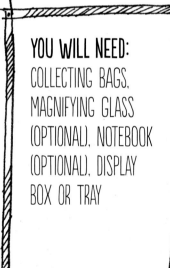

Tip: For smaller exhibits, you can use an old ice-cube tray to display your finds.

Host an outdoor Halloween feast

Wrap up warm this Halloween and you can lay on a spooky outdoor feast for your friends.

First, you need something to serve food on. If you have a garden table, give it a good wash down, as it can get quite mucky outside. If not, ask if you can bring out a table and chairs from the house.

Spooky lighting is essential – ask a grown-up to help you hollow out some pumpkins and carve some scary faces. They can then put some tea lights in for you when it starts getting dark.

Why not make a spooky centrepiece? Twigs arranged in a plant pot can create some interesting shadows at night and you can hang on some black cardboard bats for added drama.

Tomato soup is warming for a chilly evening – and very handily comes in a suitable Halloween colour. If you hollow out a medium-sized pumpkin this makes a wonderful serving bowl. Ask a grown-up to heat the soup and then you can carefully add the cobweb detail by making circles with some diluted crème fraîche or thick cream in an icing piping bag. Then, using a wooden toothpick, just draw lines across them, from the centre outwards.

YOU WILL NEED:

A TABLE, CHAIRS, PUMPKIN, TEA LIGHTS, TWIGS, PLANT POT, BLACK CARD, SCISSORS, PENCIL, TOMATO SOUP, CRÈME FRAÎCHE, ICING BAG, TOOTHPICK, LOTS OF OTHER DELICIOUSLY SPOOKY HALLOWEEN FOOD AND DRINK

Tip: If you have a chiminea or fire basket you could ask a grown-up to make you a fire to toast some ghost marshmallows.

Take a penny hike

Coins can make a family walk a lot more fun. Not because they can be used to purchase an ice cream at the end (although that's never a bad idea), but because you can let them decide the route.

Take your penny and flip it whenever you come to a junction. If it comes up heads you go left, or if it's tails, turn right. You can either keep going until you get back to where you started or you can give yourself a set time, after which you turn back and head home.

To make it more interesting, you can combine it with an A to Z spot, where you try to find something on your walk beginning with A, then B, then C and so on. Or you could split into two groups and see who gets back first. If you do this, try to record your route on a piece of paper and compare them on your return.

This is a great way to explore different areas, routes and paths you might not usually walk down. Just don't forget, if you do find yourself passing an ice-cream van, make sure you leave yourself at least one coin in the change.

YOU WILL NEED:
ONE COIN (OR MORE IF ICE CREAM IS REQUIRED), GROWN-UP TO ACCOMPANY YOU

Heads we go left, tails we go right!
Heads I dig a hole, tails I chase a cat!

Enjoy a paper bug hunt

This is the perfect bug hunt for people who are squeamish about bugs – and for bugs who are squeamish about people. In fact, it doesn't really involve bugs at all – which is good, because they have very busy schedules.

Print or colour lots of pictures of different bugs and creepy crawlies. Make sure you keep a note of each one – or even better another picture – to put on the collecting bags.

Place the bugs around the garden (or ask an adult to do it, so you can take part in the hunt). It's a nice idea to place bugs near where you would expect to find them – purple flowers for butterflies, compost bins or soil for worms, fresh green leaves for caterpillars.

Every person has a collecting bag listing all the bugs they have to find – or a picture of each (especially for younger children). On the word 'go', everyone begins hunting for their bugs. The first person to collect one of each is declared the winner and is given some snails to eat. Sorry. I meant sweets. They are given some sweets to eat. (It's an easy mistake to make.)

YOU WILL NEED:
PAPER, PRINTER AND COMPUTER OR PENS AND COLOURED PAPER, PAPER COLLECTING BAGS OR EVEN A LARGE ENVELOPE, SNAILS/SWEETS FOR THE WINNER

Tip: This makes a good party game for lots of children divided into hunting teams.

182

Go stargazing

'Twinkle twinkle little star, how I wonder what you are...'

...Oh, hang on, I do know what you are. You're Polaris, brightest star in the Ursa Minor constellation.

Yes, that's right – if you learn to stargaze, you can ruin this lullaby for everyone.

First, you'll need to be somewhere dark. If you live in a city, you may find all the streetlights make it hard to spot stars at all, but if you're visiting friends or family in less light-polluted areas, or even better, going camping, there'll be plenty of opportunities to stargaze.

Next, get comfy. It's easiest to stargaze when lying on your back, so bring out old blankets and cushions to stretch out on. You'll also need a sky chart. You can print out a free one from the Internet, buy a planisphere or borrow an astronomy book from your local library.

It's a good idea to try to find and learn about only one or two constellations at a time (you'll see some of them on the opposite page). When looking at the night sky, you'll have to imagine the lines connecting the stars but when you've learnt a couple, you'll be able to move your star map around so it lines up with the sky you're staring at.

YOU WILL NEED:
CUSHIONS AND BLANKETS,
SKY CHART, TORCH (TO
READ THE CHART)

Tip: Why not keep a stargazing diary where you can draw on the constellations you see each time, and add to it as you spot and identify more. You can also use the diary to track the different phases of the moon over a week or two and see how it changes.

Some popular constellations to look for ...

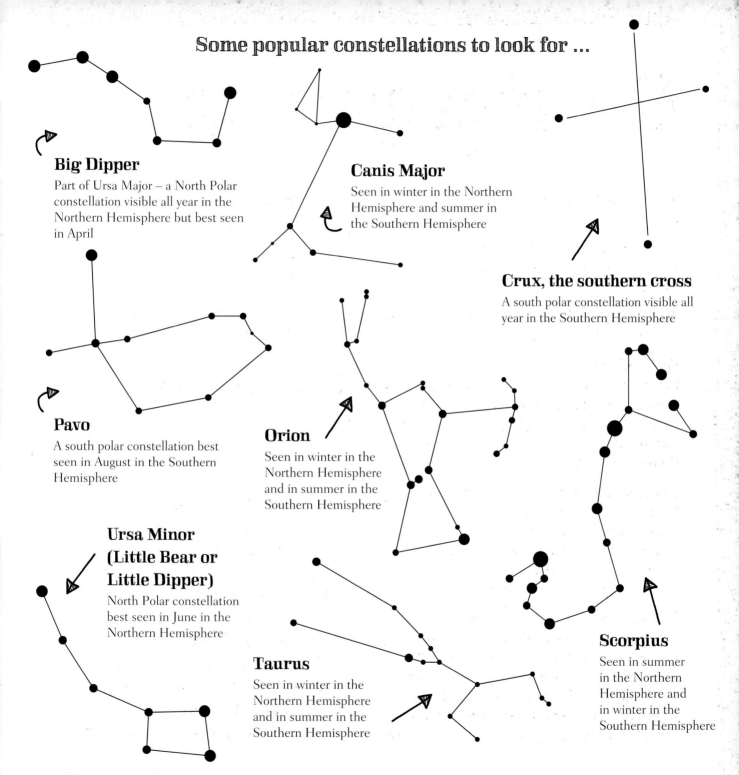

Big Dipper

Part of Ursa Major – a North Polar constellation visible all year in the Northern Hemisphere but best seen in April

Canis Major

Seen in winter in the Northern Hemisphere and summer in the Southern Hemisphere

Crux, the southern cross

A south polar constellation visible all year in the Southern Hemisphere

Pavo

A south polar constellation best seen in August in the Southern Hemisphere

Orion

Seen in winter in the Northern Hemisphere and in summer in the Southern Hemisphere

Ursa Minor (Little Bear or Little Dipper)

North Polar constellation best seen in June in the Northern Hemisphere

Scorpius

Seen in summer in the Northern Hemisphere and in winter in the Southern Hemisphere

Taurus

Seen in winter in the Northern Hemisphere and in summer in the Southern Hemisphere

NOTE: If you're in the Southern Hemisphere, you'll need to turn this page upside down for some of these constellations.

Create wellie fashion

YOU WILL NEED:
WELLIES, WASHING-UP BOWL, SOAPY WATER, SCRUBBING BRUSH, TABLE, OLD CLOTH OR NEWSPAPERS, SANDPAPER (OPTIONAL), PENCIL, OLD CLOTHES OR PAINTING APRON, ACRYLIC PAINTS OR PAINT PENS, PAINTBRUSHES, GLITTER, RIBBON, CRAFT SCISSORS, ITEMS TO ADD TO TRIM

Wellies are the Cinderellas of the footwear world. Never polished, paraded or displayed with pride. So why not play Fairy Godmother and give your boots a makeover?

First, you need to wash your wellies. Take a bucket of soapy water outside and give them a good scrub before leaving them to dry in the sun.

Now set up an outside table, covered with newspapers or an old oilcloth, and lay out your creative fashion tools such as acrylic paints, glitter and old ribbons.

If the boots are very shiny, you can give them a quick rub over with sandpaper to help the paint stick. Then just wipe off any dust with an old cloth before you start.

Mark out your pattern or design in pencil and make sure you're wearing some old clothes or a painting apron before picking up a brush and getting creative.

If you do make a mistake, quickly wipe off the paint with an old cloth or piece of kitchen towel before it has a chance to dry.

If you want to add a bit of sparkle, then sprinkle some glitter onto the paint while it's still wet.

When you've completed the design and your paint is dry (this may take a few hours if you use the paint quite thickly, but will be dry in a matter of minutes if you use acrylic paint pens), you can start adding a trim. Bend the top of the wellie over inside and cut a small slit using some craft scissors. Do this every 2–3cm until you have gone around the top of both boots. (You may need to ask a grown-up to help.)

Now take your ribbon and weave it in one slot and out of the other so that you can see the colour appearing in sections along the top of the boot. You can add more than one piece of ribbon to give you different colours and, if you want to create more interest, you can thread the ribbon through other items such as shells or stones with holes in them so that it acts like a charm bracelet. Finally, tie the ribbons in a bow at the front.

And now your Cinderella wellies are ready to go to the ball – or at least jump up and down in a few puddles.

Catch autumn leaves

YOU WILL NEED:
AUTUMN, TREES

There are many sure-fire ways to collect wishes. Extinguishing all your birthday cake candles in one go, getting the larger portion of a chicken's wishbone, or blowing away an eyelash you've found*. But if you really want to increase your wish counter, you need to go and catch some autumn leaves.

Yes, that's right. If you can catch an autumn leaf as it drops from the tree, you are granted a wish**. Unfortunately, it's not as easy as you think. A leaf tends not to text and let you know when it's going to fall. Nor does it drop in a straight line. Nope, it does that floaty, swooshy, change-my-mind-where-I'm-going-every-two-seconds kind of falling. But hey, if it was easy, we'd be inundated with wishes and before you know it there'd be no school, ice cream for every meal and Christmas occurring at least 27 times a year.

But go on, give it a go. And, while you're at it, you can get super competitive with everyone and count up to see who catches the most leaves. Because, of course, whoever does is allowed to eat as many sweets as they want until the end of the week***.

*   This might not be true.

**   This might not be true either.

***   This definitely isn't true because I've just made it up.

Balance stones

Remember stacking building blocks when you were little, and how you'd try to get them as high as you could? Well, now imagine the blocks are all different shapes and with almost no flat surfaces. Welcome to the world of stone balancing.

First, you'll need to be somewhere with a lot of stones. Beaches are always a good bet, as are rocky hillsides or even the sides of streams. Start by finding a good base stone – relatively large and flat enough that the rock won't... well... rock. Now just keep adding stones on top. You'll need to experiment and select stones carefully to keep the tower from collapsing.

If there are several of you having a go, you could compete to see who has the tallest tower, or whose is the most unusual and interesting. You could even work together on a larger stone tower more like the cairns which have been used throughout history to mark and commemorate important areas. For example: 'Here is the majestic cairn marking the very spot where Rachel beat her brother in a stone-balancing competition.' That sort of thing.

Tip: You can limit yourself to one stone per layer, or you could construct towers of stones with several forming each new storey.

YOU WILL NEED:
STONES

Play shark

Before you begin playing shark, you'll need to make some safe areas for the fishes to hide – don't worry, you won't have to build elaborate sea caves, just put out some hoops, towels, circles of skipping rope or draw chalk rings – after all, what are imaginations for?

One player is the shark whilst all the others become fishes. When the shark shouts 'swim little fishes', everyone has to leave their safe circle and try to get to another one before they are tagged by the shark. If you've been caught, you become a shark too and the game continues until the last free fish is declared the winner.

YOU WILL NEED:
SOMETHING TO CREATE 'SAFE AREAS'
E.G. HULA HOOPS, SKIPPING ROPES,
TOWELS, CHALK

Tip: If you want to make it trickier, create smaller safe areas so only one or two fishes can fit on each.

Paint rocks that rock

Considering they don't move, talk, play sports or do anything interesting, rocks can be surprisingly fun. If you set up an outdoor craft table with a protective cloth and acrylic paints or pens you can decorate them so they become permanent pieces in outdoor games and activities.

Relay race rocks

On one group of stones, paint actions such as hopping, running or skipping, on the second group of stones list the number of times such as 30, 2, 10, and finally, paint the pot luck group of stones which will include further instructions such as backwards (arrow backwards), with a friend (two people holding hands), while singing (musical note), with your tongue out (tongue), slowly (snail).

Now place your groups of rocks into three separate pots or buckets and split into two teams. Each player in a team, without looking, picks out one stone from each pot and has to complete the task (e.g. hopping 30 times while singing) before the next member of the team takes their three stones. The first team to have everyone complete a task is declared the winner.

YOU WILL NEED:
ROUNDED ROCKS, ACRYLIC PENS OR PAINTS,
PAINTING APRON OR OLD CLOTHES, OUTDOOR
TABLE, OLD CLOTH OR PLASTIC SHEET (TO
COVER TABLE), POTS OR BUCKETS

Story rocks

Paint a different item on each rock (a beach, teacher, spider, alien, castle – anything you like) and when they're dry, place them all into a large 'story' pot. Then, sitting around in a circle, the first person closes their eyes and takes out three rocks. Whatever is pictured has to become part of the story they are telling. After they've finished, the next person has a go. Alternatively, you can contribute to the same story, each taking a single stone at a time and adding this item to the tale. Perfect for campfire storytelling sessions.

Try French cricket (and hit the bucket)

Thankfully, you don't have to be French to play this game, but if you want to throw in the odd 'ooh la la' just to spice things up, then please be my guest.

You need a cricket bat (or even a tennis racket), a decent amount of space and several players. One player is chosen to bat first and must stand with their legs together whilst all the others form a wide circle a few metres away and act as both bowlers and fielders.

The 'stumps' in French cricket are the batsman's legs below the knee, so the players bowl underarm and try to hit them. The batsman defends by hitting the ball away. If he does, then he can move his feet to face in the direction the ball has landed.

The other players run to stop the ball or run and fetch it from its landing spot and this is where they bowl from next time.

When a batsman fails to hit the ball they have to keep their feet in the same spot and twist their body around to defend the 'stumps'.

If a ball is caught or the 'stumps' are hit, the batman's turn is over and the fielder who got him out takes his place.

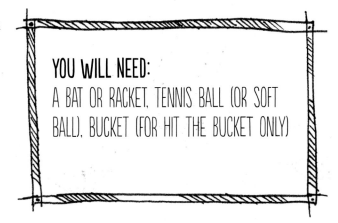

YOU WILL NEED:
A BAT OR RACKET, TENNIS BALL (OR SOFT BALL), BUCKET (FOR HIT THE BUCKET ONLY)

Build a snow lantern

YOU WILL NEED:
SNOW, WARM CLOTHES (SKI GLOVES ARE PARTICULARLY USEFUL), TEA LIGHT, TAPER, MATCHES (AND A GROWN-UP)

Tip: If you have a pathway, why not use a series of lanterns to light people's way?

Next time the weather turns wintry, how about ditching the snowball fights and having a go at creating a snow lantern instead?

First, you need to pick up some snow. Now shape it into a nice ball and then… No! Don't throw it.

Okay, let's start again.

Mould your snowball and then, just for once, resist the temptation to hurl it at someone. Instead, place it on the ground and add more balls, with a gap between each, until you make a circle.

Now add another layer of snowballs on top, bridging the gaps, but also making the circle slightly smaller.

Keep adding layers, in smaller and smaller circles until the final circle just leaves a small opening at the top which will serve as a chimney. Then push the tea light carefully through a gap between the bottom ring of snowballs until it's in the middle of your lantern.

Finally, when it's starting to get dark, ask a grown-up to come out with you to light your lanterns using a very long lit taper.

Not only will you enjoy some brilliant winter lighting but, best of all, next day, you still have a pile of snowballs pre-rolled and ready to hurl.

Make a snow labyrinth

There are times when getting lost in a maze is not much fun; if you desperately need a wee, for example, or if you're freezing cold, and particularly if you are feeling both at the same time.

So rather than making a snow maze, how about constructing a positive labyrinth? This is a fancy name for 'a maze you can't get lost in' but calling it a positive labyrinth will make you sound very clever and intimidate any adults within earshot.

First, make a snowball by patting and shaping it with your gloved hands. Then begin to roll it back and forth until it picks up snow. Pat this as you go and keep rolling until you have picked up all the snow and you can clearly see the ground beneath for a length of about a metre.

Do the same in the other direction so you have made a '+' shape. Then lean over and dig out snow with your hand to form 'dots' at the four 'corners' of this shape.

Roll another snowball until you clear a hook shape from the top of the vertical line to the top right hand corner dot. Then roll another from the far right point of your '+', round the top, until you loop back to the top left-hand dot. Next, roll from the far left point of your '+', looping over the top and back to the bottom right dot. Finally, roll the longest line down from the bottom of your '+', out to the right, over the top and back to the bottom left dot.

Now your labyrinth is complete, have a go at walking the path (or a quick jog if you need the loo).

YOU WILL NEED:
SNOW, WARM GLOVES (SKI ONES WORK WELL), CONCENTRATION

Tip: When your snowball becomes larger and is making too wide a path, throw it out beyond your labyrinth (or at someone – that's always fun) and start with a new one.

To make a labyrinth …

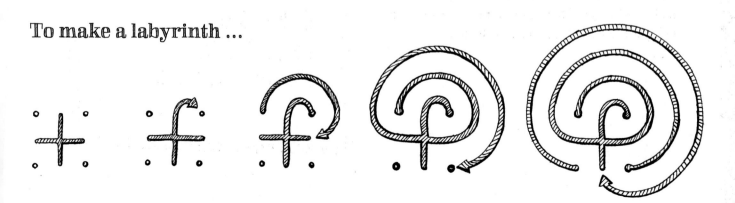

Tip: You don't need to limit yourself to igloos. The 'bricks' will form everything from castles to city walls.

Create a mini igloo

The key word here is 'mini' because, for most of us, our back gardens won't see enough snow to make an igloo door knocker, never mind an igloo. Not that they have door knockers. Or doors. But you get my point.

So instead, you can make this pint-sized dwelling. The first job is to form some bricks. Old margarine pots are perfect for this. To help strengthen them so they keep the shape better, try putting one inside another. Then simply pack the snow tightly into the tub before turning it over and giving it a hard tap. It's very similar to making sandcastles – although a lot colder. Hopefully, your brick will be loosened and come out perfectly formed and ready for construction to begin.

You can then use these bricks to form the igloo base (remembering to leave a gap for the entrance), before building them up, each layer leaning in slightly so that the igloo tapers towards the top.

The final bricks can be placed to seal the roof and any extra can be used to add an entrance tunnel.

If you want a smoother finish, you can pat extra snow on top of the structure to fill any small gaps.

YOU WILL NEED:
SNOW, MARGARINE TUBS

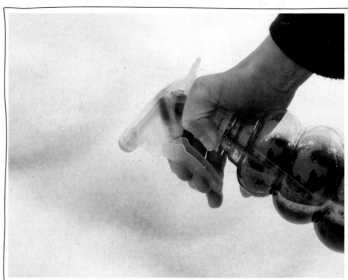

Tip: If it's a very cold day, you can even spray frosted branches and watch trees and bushes change colour.

Paint snow

The thing about snow is it's very white. Some might say too white. So why not bring some much-needed colour into the winter landscape?

First, you'll need a spray bottle – add some food colouring and dilute it with water. Just be careful not to over dilute or your colour will be very pale.

Ideally, you would have one spray bottle for each colour, but you can also rinse it out, refill it and use other colours as you go.

Now, go outside and get spraying.

You can experiment with different effects as you go. If you spray very close to the ground the colour will be stronger and the area covered smaller. Some spray bottles can also be adjusted so you can spray in smaller or larger drifts.

You can even try spraying one colour over the top of another to colour mix. For example, red sprayed over blue will create a purple area.

YOU WILL NEED:
SPRAY BOTTLES, FOOD COLOURING, WATER, SNOW

Rustle up a bird feast

You might not envy their diet of insects, nuts and seeds, but I'm sure you can sympathise with a rumbling tummy. Yes, birds can get very peckish, so why not help by setting up your own 'all you can eat' snack bar? If you don't have a handy tree from which to hang your gourmet delights, you can even make your own from some cut-off branches.

A large plant pot is a great place to house your 'fake tree'. As they don't have roots to anchor them, you will need to wedge your branches between bricks or stones to stop them flopping over. You can then fill around them with soil or sand, before adding some pretty stones to decorate around the base.

You can then make it look rather beautiful at the same time as laying out some tasty treats for the birds. Use unsalted and unbuttered popcorn threaded onto garden wire to make nibble rings. You can also add a loop to the end of some wire before threading on sliced apples. And, unlike you, the birds won't turn up their noses when the apple looks a bit brown (yeah, you might want to learn something from this).

For a really nutritious treat, get some old orange halves and thread through some more wire to hang them from the tree. You can then use one part lard (at room temperature) squished with one part flour, two parts oats and one part birdseed to make the filling. This mixture can also be smeared and pressed into old pinecones which can then be hung from the branches with some twine. And don't pull that face – I'm not asking you to eat it.

YOU WILL NEED:
CUT-OFF BRANCHES, LARGE PLANT POT, BRICKS OR STONES, SOIL OR SAND, GARDEN WIRE, UNSALTED AND UNBUTTERED POPCORN, APPLES, ORANGE HALVES, LARD, FLOUR, OATS, BIRDSEED

Tip: Birds come to rely on their regular snack bars so make sure you keep yours topped up, especially from late autumn to spring when they need it most.

Make twig stars

There's a lot you can do with twigs. Yes, I know you can use them to poke your brother. And yes, that's right, you can use them to point and laugh at your brother. Oh, OK, and to challenge your brother to a duel.

But believe it or not, you can use a twig for more than just annoying your brother.

For example, how about making some twig star decorations?

No. They are not good for throwing at your brother. Really. Sometimes I give up.

First, go hunting for some twigs. As well as old ones under trees, in late winter and early spring you might even be able to find some very colourful ones – this is the time dogwood (*Cornus*) is cut back and it has lovely red or yellow stems. It is also when you may find some pussy willow stems (*Salix caprea*) – these furry buds add a touch of glamour to your star.

First, cut or snap your twigs into six equal lengths. Arrange them into two triangles and use twine to tie them together. If you find this tricky, you could use thin garden wire instead. Then place one triangle upside down over the other to form a six-pointed star. Again, use twine (or wire) to join these where they overlap.

You can even make a five-pointed star with no twine or wire at all. First, you need a twig that is very bendable – a slender twig of willow (*Salix*) is perfect. Make the first bend at about 16–18cm from the thinner end, then another four bends at 10cm intervals. Next make a '4' shape from the first three sections, before bending back the final two pieces to form the last two points on the star. Use the excess at the end of the first section to tie the last piece in place.

If you leave a long section at the end, this star can even act as a wand. Perfect for woodland fairies.

Tip: These stars make wonderful Christmas decorations – especially if sprayed with gold, silver or white paint.

YOU WILL NEED:
TWIGS, TWINE AND/OR GARDEN WIRE

To make your star ...

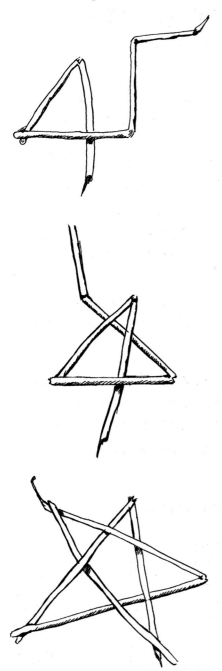

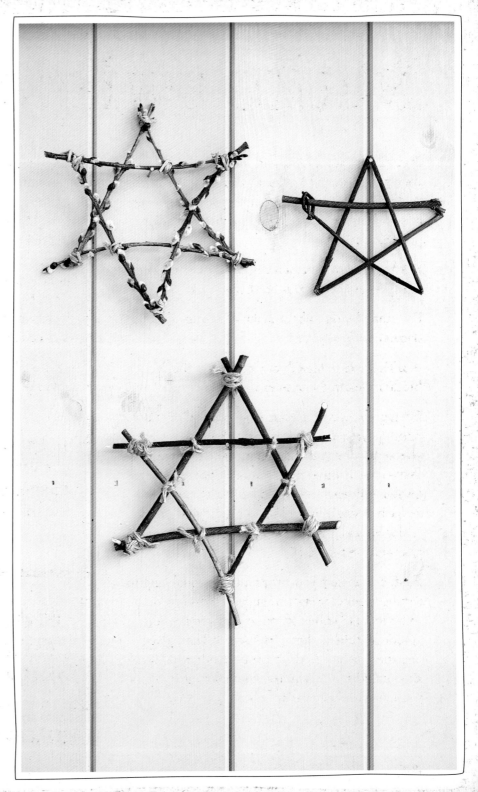

Play sky spy

So you've built rockeries, woven fences, held sports days, put on open-air plays, raced snails, spotted moths and 100 other things. I'm guessing you're feeling a little bit tired right now.

Well, find a space outside and have a lie down. Bring a blanket if you like. Are you comfy? Good.

Oi! Who said you could have a nap? Haven't you looked at the title of this book? Does it say '100 things to do outside'? No, it doesn't. We've still got one to go.

Now open your eyes, we're going to play sky spy.

Thankfully, this is a remarkably lazy game. All you need to do is spot things from your list – the only rule is that they must be in the sky when you see them. The list might differ from season to season or you could simply have to be the first to spot a certain number from the list.

For example: butterfly, bird, dragonfly, wasp, bee, fly, aeroplane, cloud.

Oh, and if a bird poops on your head, you are declared the undisputed winner and can retire from the game.

YOU WILL NEED:
BLANKET, OPEN EYES

Tip: Try not to fall asleep!

Tip: You can add some sounds to 'spot' too, such as a lawnmower, car, birdsong, cow mooing, laughter.

Resources

UK

Argos
Online or high street shops good for laminators and pouches, solar outdoor fairy lights, and many outdoor activity and game supplies.
www.argos.co.uk
0845 6403030

Baker Ross
Huge range of craft accessories including card, paints, scissors, glitter and acrylic paint pens.
www.bakerross.co.uk
0844 576 8922

B&Q
Wide selection of garden supplies including seeds, bulbs, weed control fabric, twine, bamboo canes, woodchips, gravel and stones, sand, hanging baskets and gardening tools. Also good for paint and primer, birdseed, duct tape, screw eyes, sandpaper, hooks and brackets.
www.diy.com
0845 609 6688

Dunelm Mill
Useful for oilcloths and many household items such as buckets, pegs, tea lights and much more.
www.dunelm-mill.com
0845 1656565

Field Guides
There are various field guides and nature books written specifically for children. You can also find a range of free guides to download and print on the Wildlife Watch website:
www.wildlifewatch.org.uk/spotting-sheets

Freecycle
This is a way to keep usable items out of landfill sites and is a great source of other people's unwanted items from empty jars, old tyres and hosepipes to leaking wheelbarrows and buckets. Go to www.uk.freecycle.org to find your local online group.

Garden centres
There are various garden centres across the country and you should find your local one is a good all-year-round source of gardening supplies and specialist plants such as alpines, herbs and aquatics. You can find local centres by searching The Garden Centre Association: www.gca.org.uk
0118 930 8918

Milletts
Great for outdoor equipment such as tent pegs, torches, compasses, ski gloves and binoculars.
www.millets.co.uk
0844 257 2079

Wilkinsons
Great source of good value household items such as jugs, bowls, buckets, clothes pegs, spray bottles, utensils and colanders. Also good for craft items such as double-sided sticky tape and card as well as garden supplies in season.
www.wilko.com
08456 080807

Australia

Big W
Solar outdoor fairylights, craft and game supplies.
www.bigw.com.au
1300 244 999

Bunnings Warehouse
Garden supplies and household items from bamboo canes to tea lights.
www.bunnings.com.au
038831 9777

Kmart
Home, game and garden supplies.
www.kmart.com.au
1800 124 125

Freecycle
www.freecycle.org/group/au

Categories

Quick projects (can be finished in an hour or so)

Longer projects (will take half a day, or be spread out over a few days)

Good for spring

Good for summer

Good for autumn

Good for winter

Games

Gardening projects

Craft projects

Good at the seaside

Hold a scavenger hunt (p.24)
Play tag games (p.58)
Hold a mini Olympics (p.74)
Go crabbing (p.80)
Cook with sun (p.90)
Hold a ball battle (p.104)
Explore with an underwater
  viewer (p.108)
Make a sand ball run (p.116)

Play beach games (p.132)
Fly a homemade kite (p.158)
Blow giant bubbles (p.164)
Create your own nature
  exhibit (p.176)
Go stargazing (p.184)
Balance stones (p.190)
Play shark (p.192)
Try French cricket (p.196)

Good for wildlife lovers

Build a bird hide (p.34)
Make a butterfly feeder
  (p.76)
Go crabbing (p.80)
Sweep for bugs (p.86)
Construct a stumpery (p.88)
Capture animal tracks (p.96)
Go pond dipping (p.102)
Explore with an underwater
  viewer (p.108)

Build a pitfall trap (p.118)
Trail ants (p.140)
Hold a snail race (p.144)
Make a mini wildlife pond
  (p.146)
Use a pooter (p.148)
Spot moths (p.152)
Watch worms work (p.162)
Rustle up a bird feast
  (p.206)

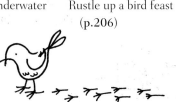

Good for livening up walks/out and about

Good in the park (no garden required)

Index

Acknowledgements

Thank you to Kyle Cathie and everyone at Kyle Books, particularly my brilliant editor, Catharine Robertson, whose support has been unwavering. My gratitude also goes to Louise Leffler for a genius book design and Sarah Leuzzi for her delightful drawings.

I am indebted to Will Heap, whose beautiful photographs have brought this book to life, and to our marvellous models in front of the camera: Maisie and Darcy Edwards; Tia Lucy Holloway; Nancy, Flora and Daphne Delfas; Stan, Scarlet and Tommy Heap; Posy and Cordelia Gulbekian Faram; Rowan and Tilly Greenwood; and Chloe and Phoebe Smith.

Thanks go to Martine Carter at Sauce Management for introducing me to Kyle and kick-starting this whole adventure and last, but never, ever least, my gratitude and love to a wonderful family: Ava, Oscar and Archie for being prepared to go outside, whatever the weather, and try out these 101 ideas, and Reuben for bucket-loads of patience and his knack for always saying the right thing.